United States
Department of
Agriculture

Forest Service

Southern
Research Station

e-General Technical
Report SRS–152

Economic Dynamics of Forests and Forest Industries in the Southern United States

Thomas J. Brandeis, Andrew J. Hartsell,
James W. Bentley, and Consuelo Brandeis

The Authors:

Thomas J. Brandeis, Supervisory Research Forester; **Andrew J. Hartsell,** Research Forester; **James W. Bentley,** Forester; and **Consuelo Brandeis,** Research Forester, U.S. Department of Agriculture Forest Service, Southern Research Station, Forest Inventory and Analysis, 4700 Old Kingston Pike, Knoxville, TN 37919.

Agricultural lands and forests dominate the southern landscape.
(photo by Andrew J. Hartsell)

March 2012

Economic Dynamics of Forests and Forest Industries in the Southern United States

Thomas J. Brandeis, Andrew J. Hartsell,
James W. Bentley, and Consuelo Brandeis

Contents

[a] All tables in this report are available in Microsoft® Excel workbook files. Upon request, these files will be supplied in the format the customer requests. The use of trade or firm names in this publication is for reader information and does not imply endorsement by the U.S. Department of Agriculture of any product or service.

Economic Dynamics of Forests and Forest Industries in the Southern United States

Thomas J. Brandeis, Andrew J. Hartsell, James W. Bentley, and Consuelo Brandeis

Abstract

This report reviews how recent (2005-present) economic conditions have accelerated mill closings and job losses, and, to a lesser extent, influenced forest management in the Southern United States. We show that the number of primary roundwood-using mills has decreased across the South since the 1970s. At the same time, mill output has increased as the production of the remaining mills has increased. In recent years, with economic conditions unfavorable and mill output decreasing, mill closings have been on the rise. Particularly hard hit have been sawmills, largely due to the precipitous decline in housing starts. There are indications that recent economic conditions are affecting the South's timberland management. We show that for many years timberland and wood volumes have been stable or increasing across the South. There has been a decrease in the number of acres harvested but an increase in the removed volume from those decreasing acres. Although the harvested acreage is decreasing, treated acreage concurrently is increasing, a trend that indicates that landowners are postponing final harvest, perhaps in anticipation of improved market conditions while investing in management activities that maintain and increase the value of their timberlands.

Keywords: Employment, FIA, forest industry production, forest inventory, timberland management, recession, timber product output.

Introduction

The forests of the Southern United States are a vast and rich resource, not only for the region but also for the Nation, and for the world as well. Spanning 13 Southern States from Texas to Virginia, the forests include a diversity of dynamic landscapes and ecosystems, and play a vital role in the region's culture and economy. The forests are highly productive, providing raw materials that fuel regional, national, and global economies.

Southern forests, known as the "wood basket" of the Nation, accounted for 58 percent of the total timber volume harvested in the United States in 2007 (Smith and others 2009). Primary wood-processing plants in the South produced 53 percent of the saw-log and veneer products,

72 percent of the pulpwood, and 58 percent of all other roundwood products in the Nation at that time (Smith and others 2009). The South's forests are so productive that, while they makeup only 2 percent of the global forest cover, they produce 12 percent of the world's industrial roundwood and 19 percent of its pulp and paper products—greater production than that of any other nation (Smith and others 2009, Food and Agriculture Organization 2011).

Southern forests play an integral role in the region's economy and in the economy of the region's communities. As of 2008, wood-related manufacturing represents 8 percent of all manufacturing income and 10 percent of all manufacturing employment in the South (Abt 2011). In this respect, the components of environment and economy across the Southern United States are dynamically linked, with change in either component often precipitating change in the other.

Besides economic hardship for the region and affected communities across the region, losses in productivity of the South's forest industry can have negative consequences for the Nation's capacity to meet demand for wood products. Additionally, changes in timber demand may lead to different forest management practices and ownership patterns, which in turn may alter forest ecosystems. Defining and understanding these relationships is important to policy decisions that may impact the Nation's long-term economic and environmental health.

In this report, we examine how the South's forest industry has responded to long- and short-term economic conditions, and how trends might differ for pulp and sawn wood products subsectors, as well as for softwoods versus hardwoods. We also consider the economic consequences of these trends in terms of employment and income for the State economies affected by these changes. Finally, we study the response to these trends by forest landowners and managers and how these responses shape the forests of the South.

Data Sources and Methods

The data used in this report come primarily from three sources. Timber product output (TPO) data and forest inventory data come from the Forest Inventory and Analysis (FIA) program of the Forest Service, U.S. Department of Agriculture. The FIA program is a continuing endeavor mandated by the U.S. Congress, per the Forest and Rangeland Renewable Resources Planning Act of 1974 and the McSweeney-McNary Forest Research Act of 1928. The primary FIA objective is to determine the extent, condition, volume, growth, and depletion of timber on the Nation's forest land. Forest Service regional research stations are responsible for conducting these inventories and publishing summary reports for individual States. The Southern Research Station FIA program collects, compiles, and analyses the data for the States of Alabama, Arkansas, Florida, Georgia, Kentucky, Louisiana, Mississippi, North Carolina, Oklahoma, South Carolina, Tennessee, Texas, and Virginia. Information on employment, labor income, and the economic effects of the forestry sector on Southern States' economies was derived from the IMpact analysis for PLANning (IMPLAN) economic modeling software and datasets. The following sections describe each dataset and how it was assembled in more detail.

Timber Product Output in the South

This report contains data from canvasses of primary wood-using plants. The canvasses were conducted periodically in the 13 Southern States and present changes in product output by year of survey, species group, and product. The canvasses determined the amount and source of wood receipts and annual timber product drain by county as well as interstate and cross-regional movement of industrial roundwood. Only primary wood-using mills were canvassed, and statewide totals by product are reported. More detailed information on statewide and county-level TPO output is available on the online TPO database and in the individual State TPO reports summarized in Bentley (2003) and Johnson and others (2006, 2008a, 2008b, 2009, 2011). Primary mills are those that process roundwood in log or bolt form or as chipped roundwood. Examples of industrial roundwood products are saw logs, pulpwood, veneer logs, poles, posts, and logs used for composite board products. Mills producing products from residues generated at primary or secondary processors were not canvassed. Trees chipped in the woods were included only if they were delivered to a primary domestic manufacturer.

A canvass of the primary wood processors was conducted for each of the years reported. The first canvasses in the South for timber products other than pulpwood were completed in the 1930s, with subsequent canvasses made periodically for each of the Southern States. Mills were canvassed by mail or through personal contact at plant locations. Telephone contacts followed mailed questionnaire responses when additional information or clarification of response was necessary. In the event of a nonresponse, data collected in previous surveys were updated by current data collected for mills of similar size, product type, and location. Incorporated into State production estimates were data on roundwood from mills located outside of the canvassed State but known to use roundwood harvested from the canvassed State. Pulpwood production data were taken from an annual canvass of all southern pulpmills. Medium density fiberboard, insulation board, and hardboard plants were included in this survey.

Economic Data

For the economic analysis, we make use of the IMpact analysis for PLANning (IMPLAN) Version 3.0 economic modeling tools and associated datasets for 2004, 2006, 2007, 2008, and 2009 (Minnesota IMPLAN Group, Inc. 2009). All estimated dollar values are shown in 2010 dollars. IMPLAN's built-in economic multipliers are used to assess an industry's direct, indirect, and induced economic impacts. Direct effects for the sector analysis indicate total sales by the forest industry. Likewise, in the present setting, indirect effects should be interpreted as total sales by the sector's supply chain. Induced effects involve the impacts resulting from the changes in household expenditures caused by the change in production from the direct effects (changes in household income). Total effects represent the entire contribution of the forest sector industries to the study area. For each of these impact effects, IMPLAN generates estimates for employment (includes both full- and part-time jobs), labor income, output, and total value added. Output represents the industry's total value of production. An industry's value added is the difference between the total output and the costs of intermediate inputs. In other words, value added is the industry's gross contribution to an area's overall economy. In the following sections, we present the forest sector's direct and total effect on employment, labor income, and output for each of the States in the Southern Region. Table 1 presents the North American industry classification system and IMPLAN sectors used for these analyses. IMPLAN analyses include primary and secondary wood product industries, while the TPO assessments include only primary industries.

Table 1—Description of the forest sector industry groups

Forest sector group	NAICS 2007 code	IMPLAN sector	Description
Inputs	1131-2	15	Forestry, forest products, and timber tract production
	1133	16	Commercial logging
Primary			
Solid, primary	3211	95	Sawmills and wood preservation
Panel	321211-2	96	Veneer and plywood manufacturing
	321219	98	Reconstituted wood product manufacturing
Pulp and paper	32211	104	Pulpmills
	32212	105	Paper mills
	32213	106	Paperboard mills
Secondary			
Solid, secondary	321213-4	97	Engineered wood member and truss manufacturing
	32191	99	Wood windows and doors and millwork manufacturing
	32192	100	Wood container and pallet manufacturing
	321991	101	Manufactured home (mobile home) manufacturing
	321992	102	Prefabricated wood building manufacturing
	321999	103	All other miscellaneous wood product manufacturing
	33711	295	Wood kitchen cabinet and countertop manufacturing
	337122	297	Nonupholstered wood household furniture manufacturing
	337129	300	Wood television, radio, and sewing machine cabinet manufacturing
	337211-12	301	Office furniture and custom architectural woodwork and millwork manufacturing
Pulp and paper products	32221	107	Paperboard container manufacturing
	322221-2	108	Coated and laminated paper, packaging paper and plastics film manufacturing
	322223-6	109	All other paper bag and coated and treated paper manufacturing
	32223	110	Stationery product manufacturing
	322291	111	Sanitary paper product manufacturing
	322299	112	All other converted paper product manufacturing

NAICS = North American industry classification system; IMPLAN = IMpact analysis for PLANning.

Forest Inventory Data

The FIA program maintains a network of forest inventory and monitoring plots on a systematic grid across the United States. These plots are revisited and remeasured at intervals ranging from 5 to 10 years, depending on the State. Details on this program are given by Bechtold and Patterson (2005). Once compiled and processed, the data are posted to the FIA database (FIADB). The data used in this report were obtained from FIADB between January 30 and February 7, 2012.

The FIADB available to the public was developed to provide as much information as possible consistently among States. Before 1999, all inventories were conducted on a periodic basis. The 1998 Farm Bill requires FIA to collect data annually on plots in each State. A number of inventories conducted prior to the implementation of the annual inventory are available in the FIADB, but various data attributes may be empty or the items may have been collected or computed differently. Annual inventories now use a common plot design and common data collection procedures nationwide, ensuring greater consistency among the inventories by FIA work units. Data field definitions note inconsistencies caused by different sampling designs and processing methods. Detailed information on FIADB structure and FIA methodology is available in the FIADB Users Manual (Woudenberg and others 2010) and on the FIA national program—tools and data Web page (http://www.fia.fs.fed.us/tools-data/tutorials_training/default.asp).

The values presented for a given survey year represent an average over the entire survey cycle for the State. As examples the 2010 timber removal estimate for Alabama is the average of removal estimates from plots measured from 2004 to 2010 because Alabama is on a 7-year remeasurement cycle, and the 2010 removal estimate for Arkansas is the average of plot measurements made from 2006 to 2010 because Arkansas is on a 5-year remeasurement cycle. The averaging across multiple years will tend to smooth over sudden increases or decreases in estimated values when the estimate is averaged from measurements taken in years before and/or after these relatively short-term perturbations occurred. Details of the averaging calculations can be found in Scott and others (2005).

Dot Map Methodology

The dot density maps in this report represent county-level information. Each dot, randomly placed by geographic information software, represents a specific value: 50,000 cubic feet for the maps depicting total TPO production, 10,000 cubic feet for change in TPO production, and a dot for each mill or job (in the maps on mill numbers and job changes). For example, a county with two green dots represents 100,000 cubic feet of softwood production for that county (fig. 1). Thus, counties with higher concentrations of dots have greater production. Dot density figures representing change have both red and blue dots. Red dots are placed in counties that experienced a loss for the specific period, while blue dots are placed in those counties that featured gains. The

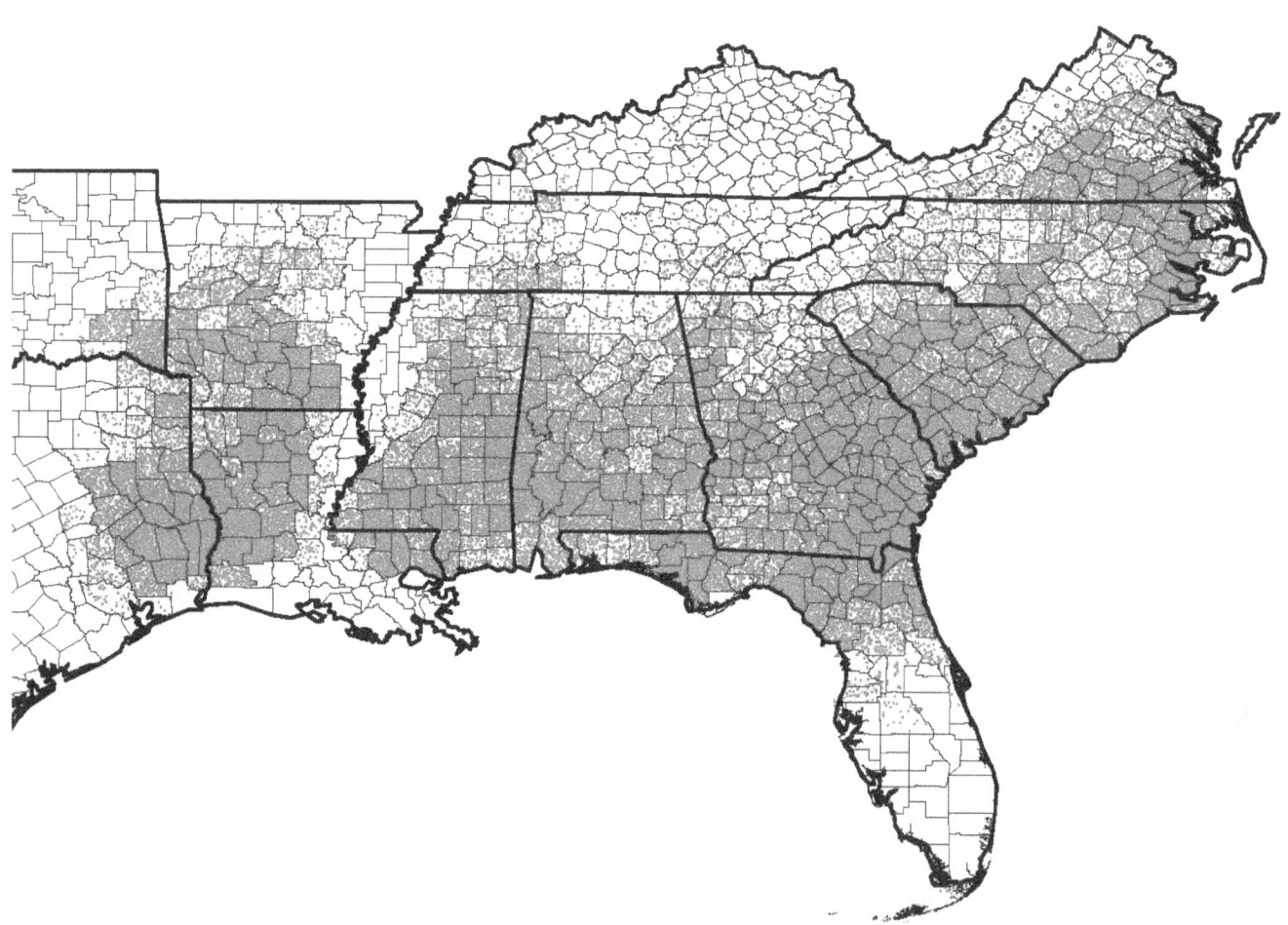

Figure 1—Total production of softwood products as derived by timber product output survey, Southern United States, 2009. Each dot represents 50,000 cubic feet of live-tree volume.

same red/blue symbology is used in the change in number of mills map (see fig. 16) and employment change map (see fig. 20), except each dot represents either one mill or one person.

Timber Product Output Trends

Long- and short-term trends in the South's timber products sector can be viewed in two ways: (1) as output of industrial timber products, and (2) as the number of primary wood-using mills producing those products. Figures 1 and 2 present the total output of all softwood and hardwood products in the Southern United States in 2009 and its distribution by State and county. Total softwood TPO across the region reached a historical high of 6.39 billion cubic feet in 2005. After that survey, there was an observed output decrease

(table 2, fig. 3) that was particularly sharp for total softwood product output, which fell to 4.97 billion cubic feet in 2009, and that produced an overall loss of 22 percent of production from 2005 to 2009. Total hardwood output followed a pattern similar to that of softwood output but had been increasing more gradually to a peak in the 1995 survey of 2.6 billion cubic feet (fig. 3). Hardwood product output then remained relatively stable until slowly decreasing to 2009 levels (fig. 3). There was still a notable decrease in total hardwood output from 2005 to 2009 surveys, with output at 1.6 billion cubic feet.

By distinguishing between saw-log and pulpwood production, we gain further insight into product output trends. Both softwood and hardwood saw-log production

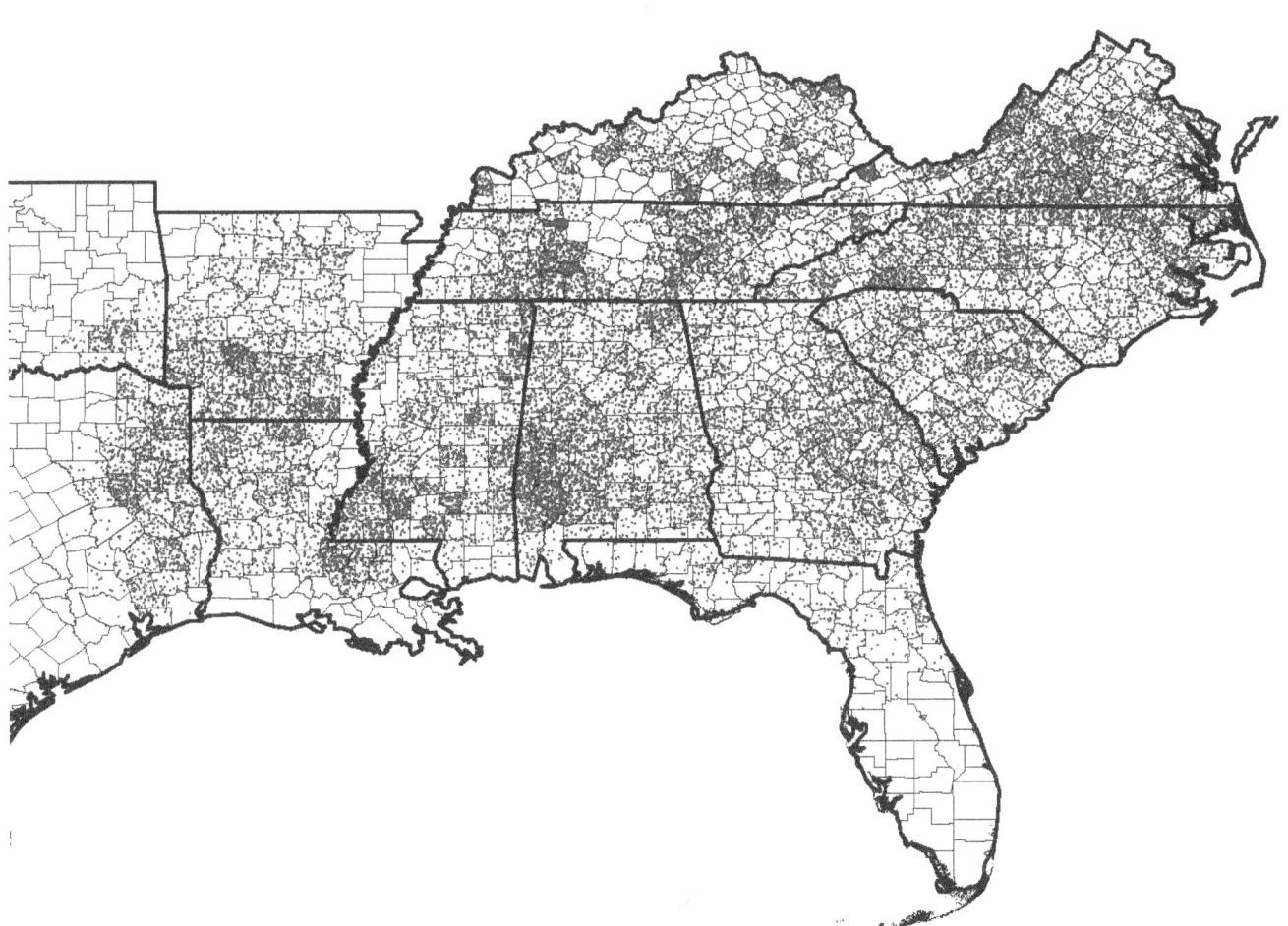

Figure 2—Total production of hardwood products as derived by timber product output survey, Southern United States, 2009. Each dot represents 50,000 cubic feet of live-tree volume.

Table 2—Output of industrial products by product, species group, and year, Southern Region

Product and species group	Year				
	1999	2003	2005	2007	2009
	thousand cubic feet				
Saw logs					
Softwood	2,731,094	2,667,325	2,887,854	2,524,468	1,642,327
Hardwood	1,008,035	985,455	997,509	922,992	615,940
Total	3,739,129	3,652,780	3,885,363	3,447,460	2,258,267
Veneer logs					
Softwood	798,960	744,141	765,727	559,076	350,042
Hardwood	97,771	85,693	80,546	65,826	34,326
Total	896,731	829,834	846,273	624,902	384,368
Pulpwood[a]					
Softwood	2,423,108	2,229,030	2,308,247	2,449,972	2,519,519
Hardwood	1,325,752	1,055,814	1,145,601	1,102,558	913,065
Total	3,748,860	3,284,844	3,453,848	3,552,530	3,432,584
Composite panels					
Softwood	160,193	268,858	342,686	469,770	322,060
Hardwood	73,040	58,284	54,356	30,635	8,664
Total	233,233	327,142	397,042	500,405	330,724
Other industrial					
Softwood	89,297	98,717	84,340	83,498	138,831
Hardwood	5,474	1,800	2,535	8,513	20,213
Total	94,771	100,517	86,875	92,011	159,044
All industrial					
Softwood	6,202,652	6,008,071	6,388,854	6,086,784	4,972,779
Hardwood	2,510,072	2,187,046	2,280,547	2,130,524	1,592,208
Total	8,712,724	8,195,117	8,669,401	8,217,308	6,564,987

[a] Includes roundwood delivered to nonpulpmills, then chipped and sold to pulpmills (76,328,000 cubic feet in 1999, 60,731,000 cubic feet in 2003, 58,540,000 cubic feet in 2005, 37,604,000 cubic feet in 2007, and 43,983,000 cubic feet in 2009).

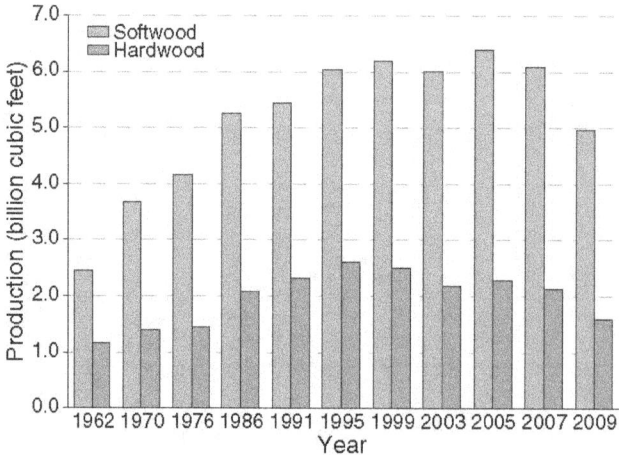

Figure 3—Roundwood production for all products by species group and year in the South.

show a gradual increase until the mid-1990s, followed by a period of relative stability prior to decreases in 2007 and 2009 (fig. 4). Softwood saw-log production decreased by 43 percent from 2005 (2.89 billion cubic feet) to 2009 (1.64 billion cubic feet), and the loss of production across the South is evident in figures 5 and 6. Hardwood saw-log production was relatively stable from 2001 to 2005 (fig. 7), but then dropped 38 percent from 2005 (1.00 billion cubic feet) to 2009 (0.61 billion cubic feet, fig. 8).

Pulpwood production trends, particularly for softwoods, have been somewhat different from the trends observed in saw-log production. Hardwood pulpwood production reached its highest levels in the 1995 survey (1.49 billion cubic feet) and

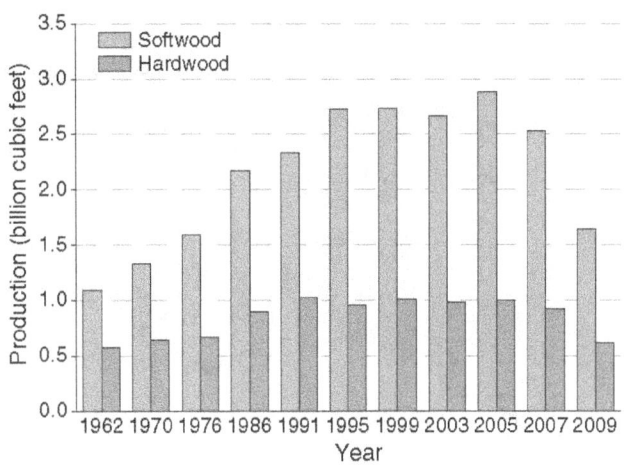

Figure 4—Roundwood saw-log production by species group and year in the South.

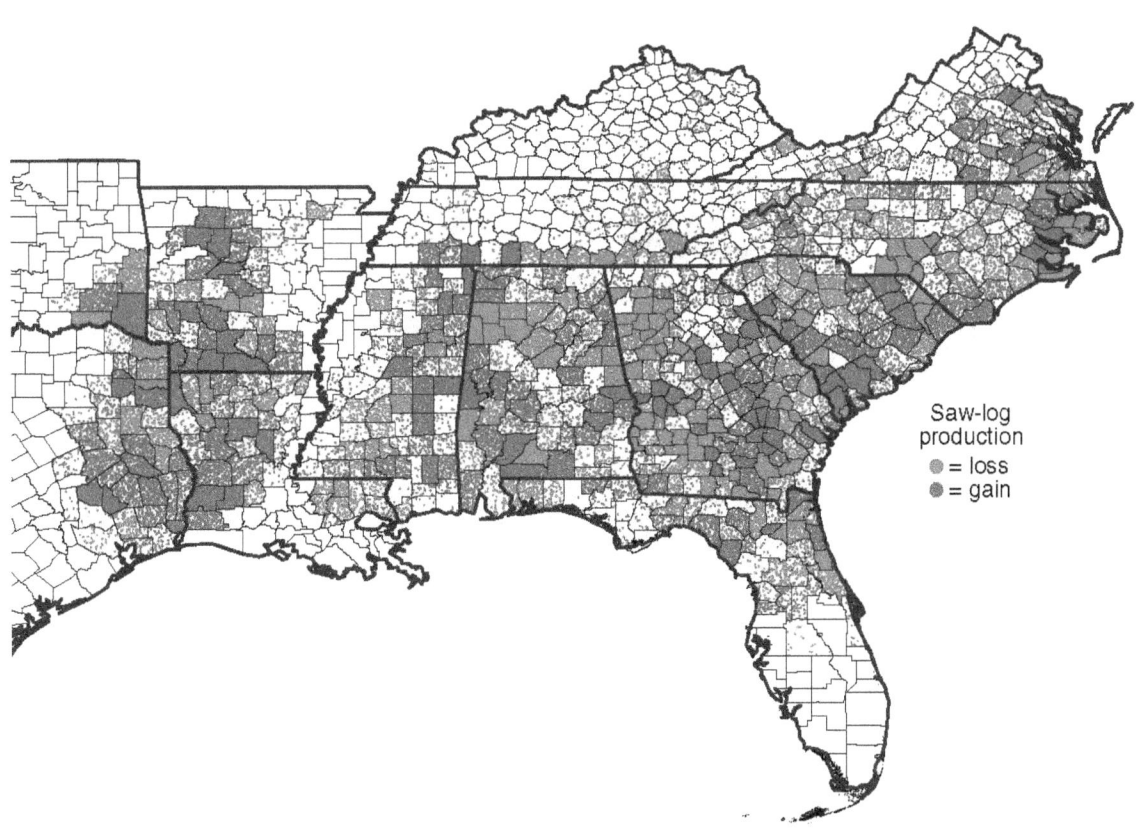

Figure 5—Total change in softwood saw-log production as derived by timber product output survey, Southern United States, 2001–05. Each dot represents 10,000 cubic feet of change.

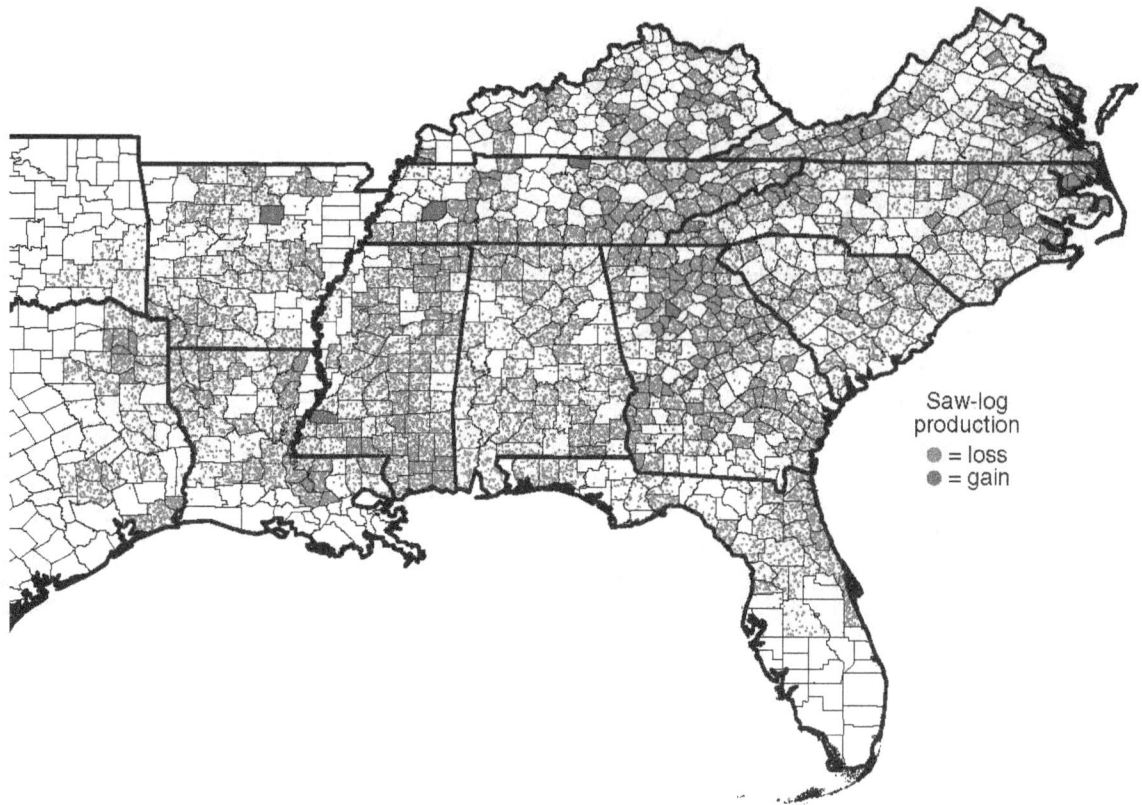

Figure 6—Total change in softwood saw-log production as derived by timber product output survey, Southern United States, 2005–09. Each dot represents 10,000 cubic feet of change.

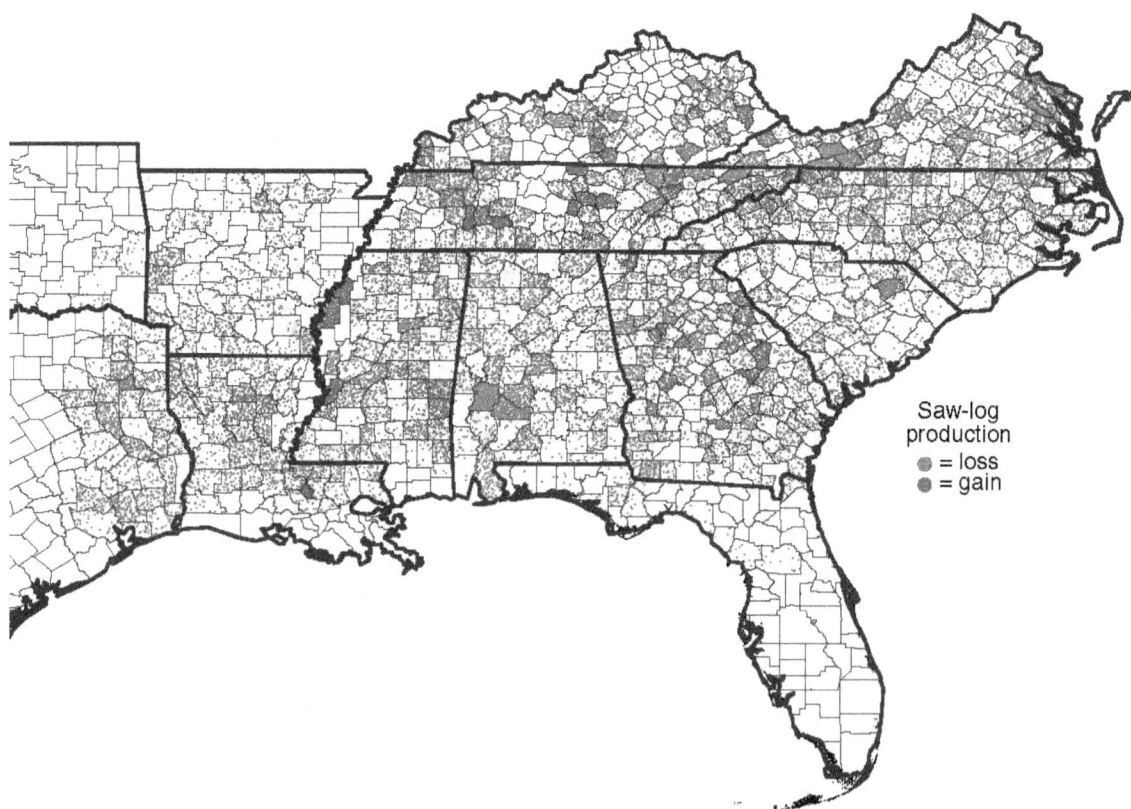

Figure 7—Total change in hardwood saw-log production as derived by timber product output survey, Southern United States, 2001–05. Each dot represents 10,000 cubic feet of change.

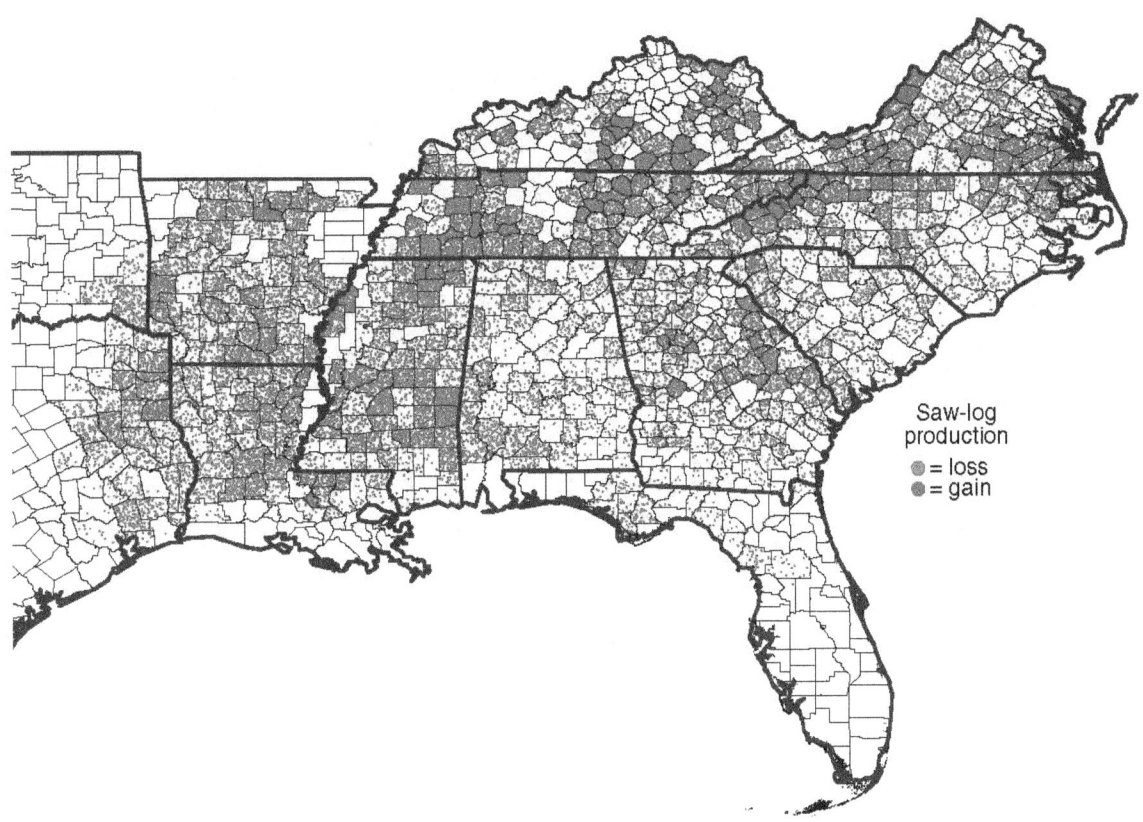

Figure 8—Total change in hardwood saw-log production as derived by timber product output survey, Southern United States, 2005–09. Each dot represents 10,000 cubic feet of change.

then gradually decreased to 0.91 billion cubic feet in 2009 (figs. 9, 10, 11). Softwood pulpwood production, however, grew and has remained relatively stable (except for dips in 2003 and 2005) through to the 2009 survey, ranging from 2.21 to 2.52 billion cubic feet since 1986 (fig. 9). Figures 12 and 13 depict the losses and gains in softwood pulpwood production between 2001 and 2009.

The decreases in saw-log and pulpwood outputs are also reflected in the production figures for other products. Softwood and hardwood veneer log production decreased 54 and 57 percent, respectively, from 2005 to 2009 (table 2). Hardwood composite panel production, while a lesser product in the overall southern forest sector, decreased 84 percent from 2005 to 2009 (table 2). Tables A.1–A.13 show detailed histories of industrial roundwood output by State, species group (softwood vs. hardwood), and product type.

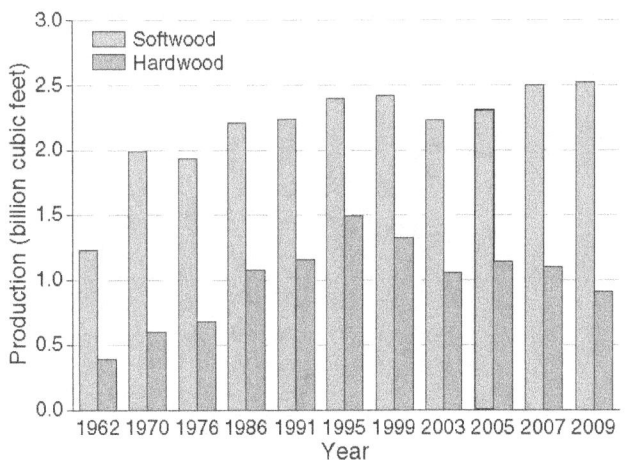

Figure 9—Roundwood pulpwood production by species group and year in the South.

9

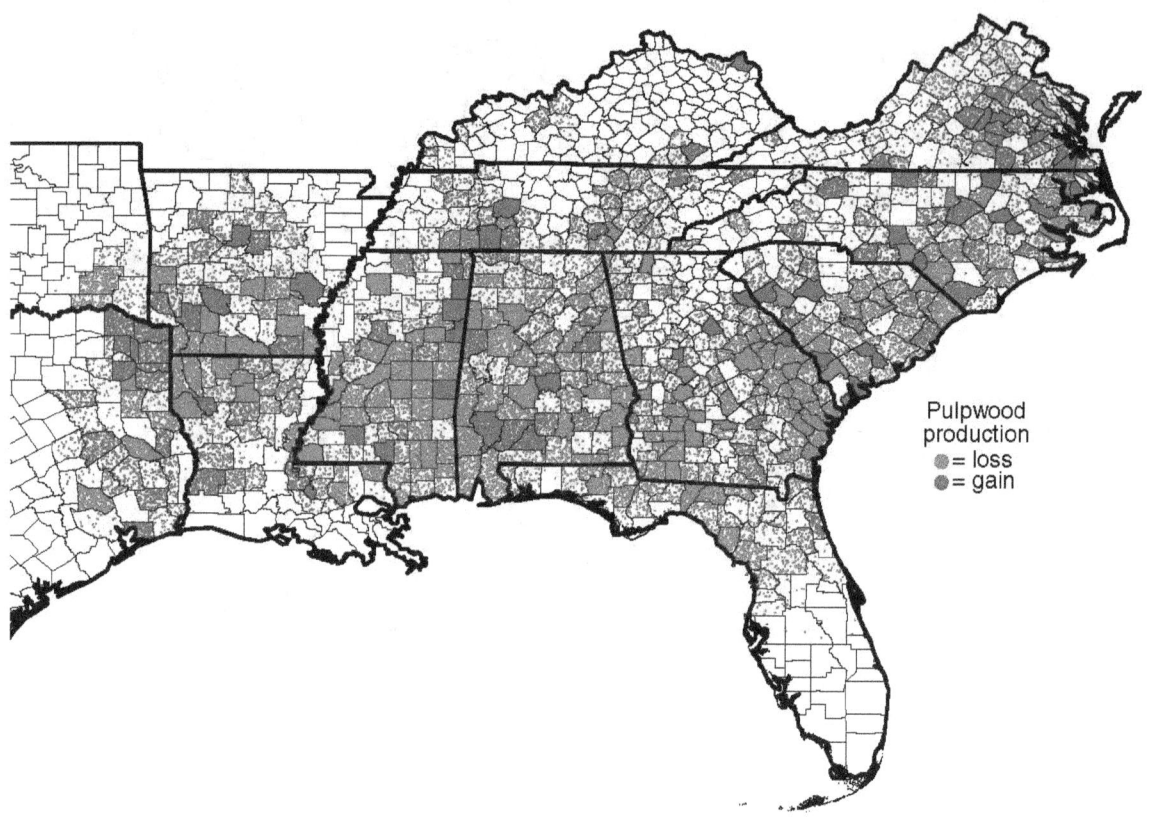

Figure 10—Total change in hardwood pulpwood production as derived by timber product output survey, Southern United States, 2001–05. Each dot represents 10,000 cubic feet of change.

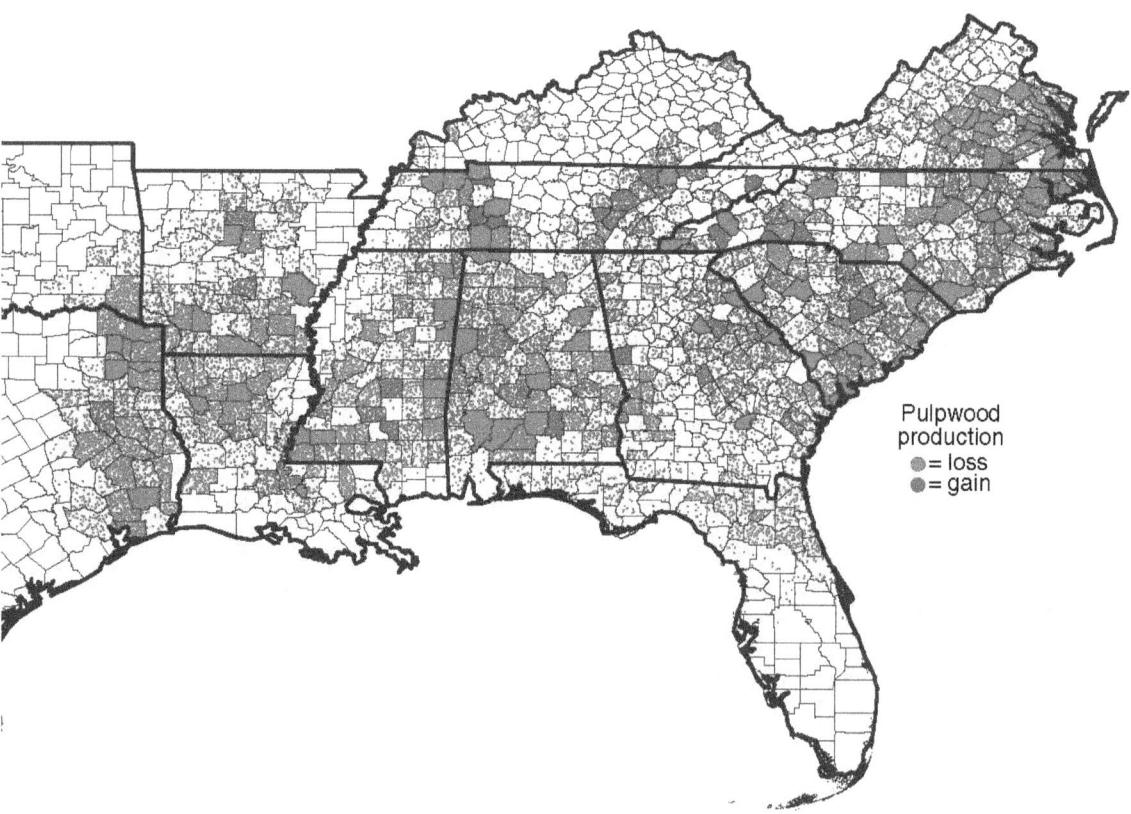

Figure 11—Total change in hardwood pulpwood production as derived by timber product output survey, Southern United States, 2005–09. Each dot represents 10,000 cubic feet of change.

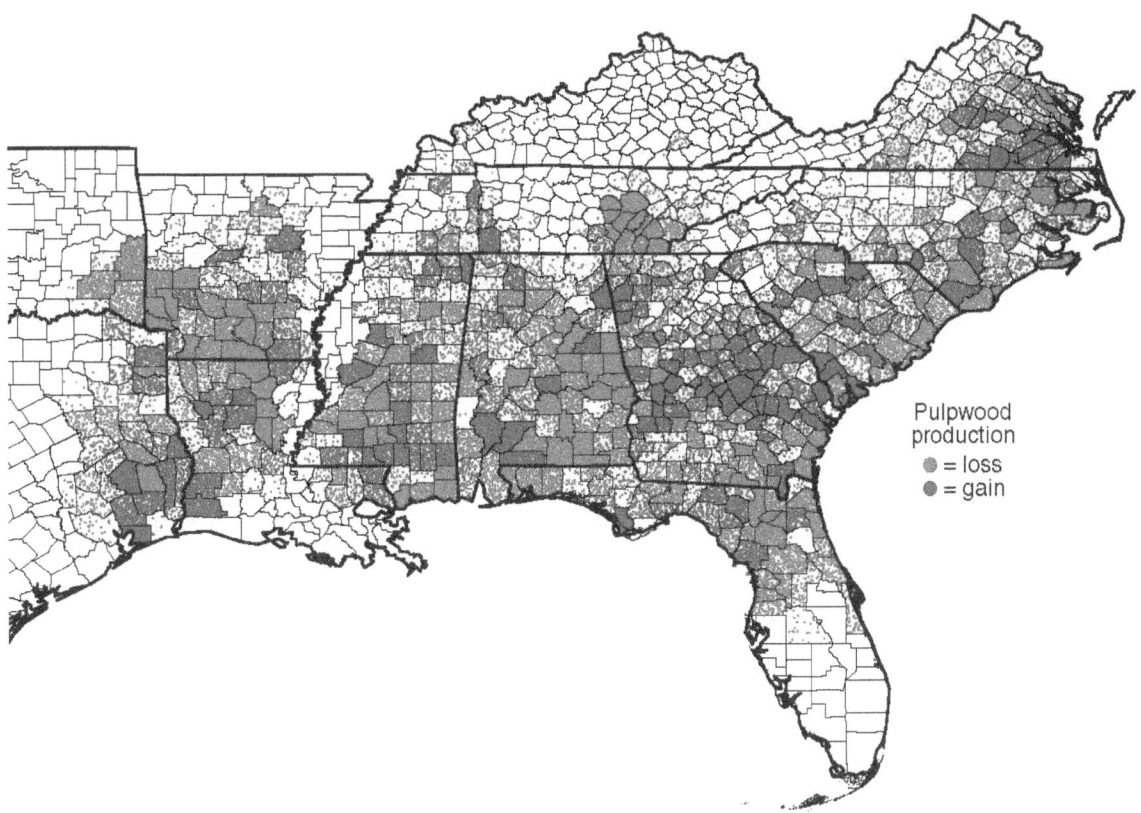

Figure 12—Total change in softwood pulpwood production as derived by timber product output survey, Southern United States, 2001–05. Each dot represents 10,000 cubic feet of change.

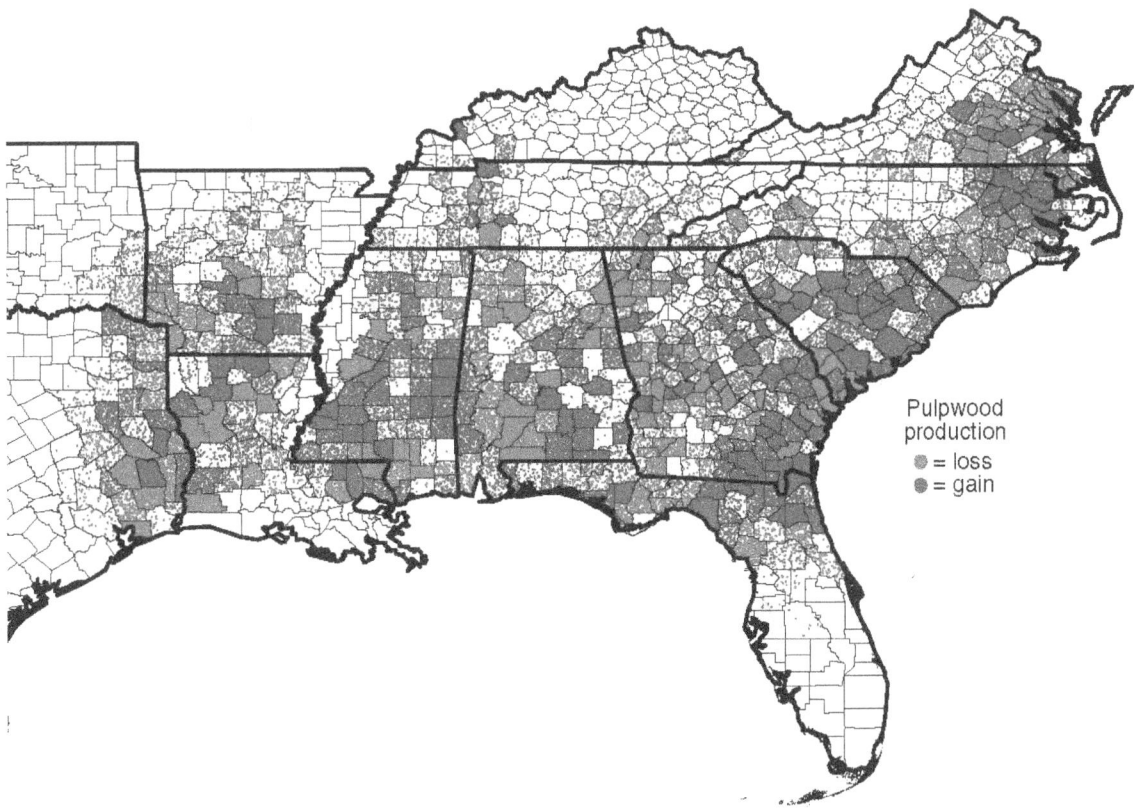

Figure 13—Total change in softwood pulpwood production as derived by timber product output survey, Southern United States, 2005–09. Each dot represents 10,000 cubic feet of change.

Number of Primary Wood-Using Plants in the Southern Region

In contrast to the increase in industrial product output described above, the total number of primary roundwood-using mills in the Southern United States has been declining since the 1970s (table 3, fig. 14). The decrease in the number of mills has varied by product produced. The number of pulpmills across the South has declined slowly while the number of sawmills has declined steadily (fig. 15). Mill losses continue to impact the local economies across the Southern United States with a net loss of 499 mills from 2005 to 2009 (fig. 16).

Table 3—Number of primary wood-using plants by type of mill, Southern Region, 1970 to 2009

Type of mill	Year										
	1970	1975	1980	1985	1990	1995	1999	2003	2005	2007	2009
	number										
Sawmills	4,289	3,591	3,482	3,086	2,683	2,386	2,165	1,931	1,669	1,540	1,216
Veneer mills	239	200	192	168	155	139	124	107	99	87	66
Pulpmills	109	115	116	107	105	105	97	91	87	87	83
Composite panel mills	0	0	0	6	11	21	24	29	30	27	24
Other mills	452	358	313	295	235	161	141	163	143	141	140
All plants	5,089	4,264	4,103	3,662	3,189	2,812	2,551	2,321	2,028	1,882	1,529

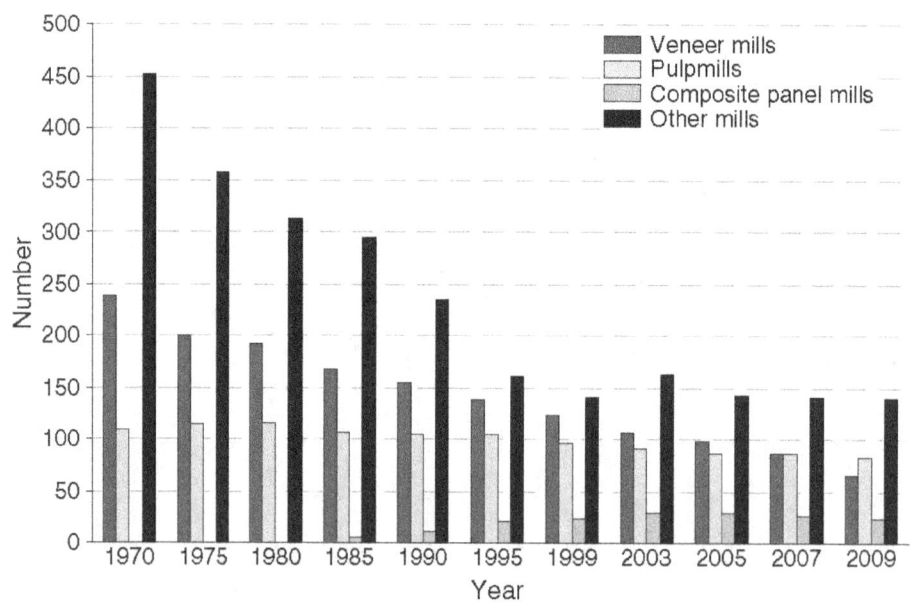

Figure 14—Number of primary wood-using plants by year and type of mill, Southern Region.

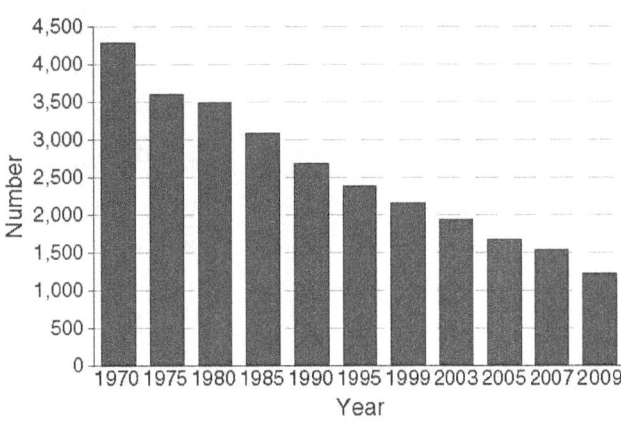

Figure 15—Number of sawmills by year, Southern Region.

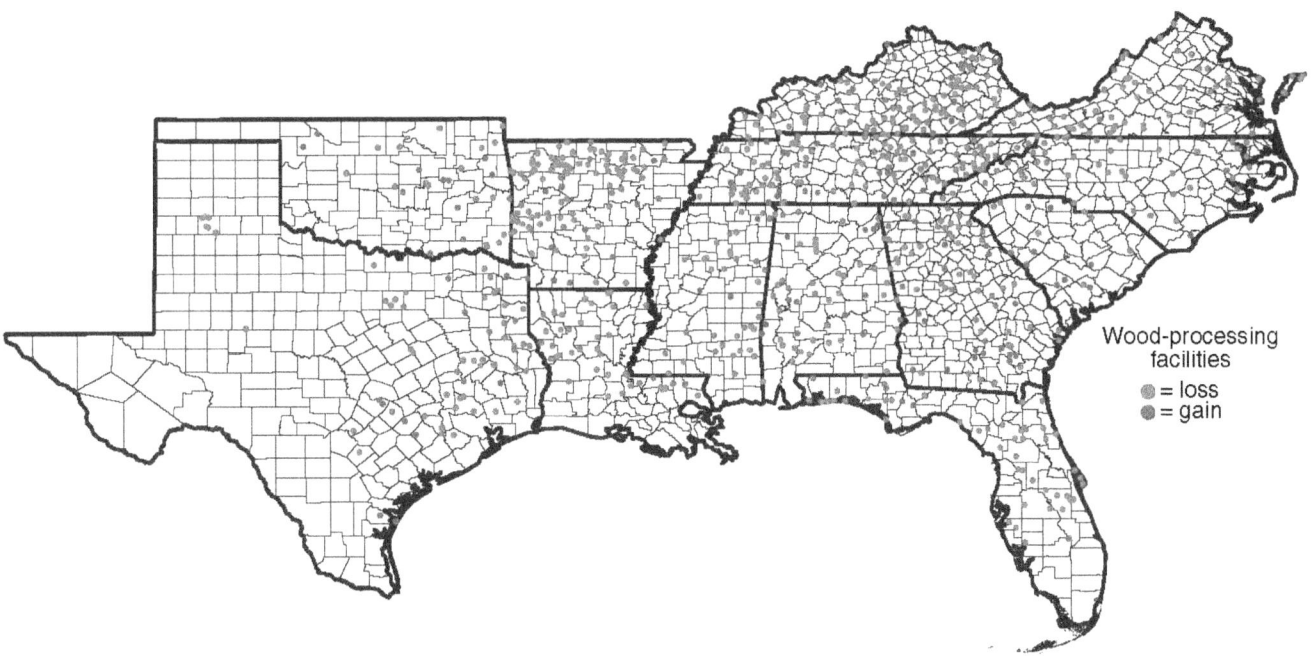

Wood-processing
facilities
● = loss
● = gain

Figure 16—Total change in the number of primary wood-processing facilities as derived by timber product output survey, Southern United States 2005–09. Each dot represents one mill.

Impacts on Jobs and Incomes

Jobs and their associated labor income are lost when mills close or curtail operations. From 2004 to 2009, the South lost 26 percent of full- and part-time jobs (direct employment), resulting in an estimated 20 percent loss in total jobs associated with the wood products industry (direct, indirect, and induced employment) (table 4, fig. 17). All Southern States showed direct job losses, varying from a low of 15 percent in South Carolina to a high of 35 percent in North Carolina (figs. 18 and 19). These job losses had a correspondingly negative effect on labor income for the Southern States (table 4). Direct job losses were particularly

acute in wood product industries that produced primary solid wood products (34 to 36 percent between 2004 and 2009) and solid secondary wood products (34 percent loss) (table 4, fig. 20).

In 2004, the total economic value of production of the South's forest primary and secondary products industries was estimated at $250.70 billion, of which $168.90 billion came directly from the goods produced by the forest industry (table 4). By 2009, the value of the sector's contribution to States' economies had decreased by 20 and 24 percent, respectively (table 4). Tables A.27–A.35 show details by State on employment, wages, and output.

Table 4—Forest sector direct and total effect in employment, labor income, and output, Southern Region, 2004–09

Forest sector group	Effect	2004	2006	2007	2008	2009	Change	Change
				Year				

Employment

- - - - - - - - - - - - - - - - number of jobs (full- and part-time) - - - - - - - - - - - - - - - -   *percent*

Forest sector group	Effect	2004	2006	2007	2008	2009	Change	Change (percent)
Inputs	Direct	64,545	66,393	72,156	73,067	59,692	-4,853	-8
	Total	182,583	190,312	141,902	166,263	120,395	-62,188	-34
Solid, primary	Direct	68,384	70,851	58,171	58,771	45,276	-23,108	-34
	Total	117,122	120,119	101,731	97,802	82,113	-35,010	-30
Panel	Direct	35,817	37,433	34,503	33,120	22,978	-12,839	-36
	Total	60,619	63,798	60,393	55,399	40,243	-20,376	-34
Pulp and paper	Direct	64,295	60,653	59,317	60,125	54,710	-9,584	-15
	Total	226,493	205,772	236,963	218,827	226,040	-453	0
Solid, secondary	Direct	230,786	245,874	230,379	232,188	151,392	-79,394	-34
	Total	357,028	396,523	410,012	389,086	266,535	-90,493	-25
Pulp and paper products	Direct	109,411	106,069	100,948	101,124	91,077	-18,333	-17
	Total	262,943	249,211	254,979	248,409	227,689	-35,253	-13
Total	Direct	573,237	587,274	555,475	558,394	425,125	-148,111	-26
	Total	1,206,788	1,225,734	1,205,980	1,175,786	963,015	-243,773	-20

Labor income

- millions of dollars -   *percent*

Forest sector group	Effect	2004	2006	2007	2008	2009	Change	Change (percent)
Inputs	Direct	$3,156	$2,853	$3,026	$3,225	$2,662	$-494	-16
	Total	6,768	6,570	5,400	6,439	4,792	-1,976	-29
Solid, primary	Direct	3,000	3,108	2,575	2,646	2,043	-957	-32
	Total	5,029	5,214	4,461	4,351	3,649	-1,380	-27
Panel	Direct	1,891	1,929	1,799	1,754	1,282	-609	-32
	Total	2,915	3,061	2,936	2,736	2,028	-887	-30
Pulp and paper	Direct	6,925	7,207	6,795	7,125	6,030	-894	-13
	Total	14,253	13,885	15,143	14,731	14,041	-213	-1
Solid, secondary	Direct	9,329	10,739	9,282	9,464	6,364	-2,965	-32
	Total	14,731	17,398	17,331	16,486	11,414	-3,317	-23
Pulp and paper products	Direct	7,680	8,038	7,484	7,599	6,390	-1,289	-17
	Total	14,605	14,608	14,679	14,569	12,702	-1,903	-13
Total	Direct	31,981	33,874	30,960	31,814	24,771	-7,209	-23
	Total	58,301	60,737	59,951	59,313	48,625	-9,676	-17

Output

- millions of dollars -   *percent*

Forest sector group	Effect	2004	2006	2007	2008	2009	Change	Change (percent)
Inputs	Direct	$22,981	$21,950	$20,708	$19,306	$9,764	$-13,217	-58
	Total	32,188	31,160	26,731	27,339	15,117	-17,071	-53
Solid, primary	Direct	19,114	19,520	16,731	14,559	10,379	-8,735	-46
	Total	25,383	26,253	22,456	19,796	15,100	-10,283	-41
Panel	Direct	7,682	9,877	9,061	8,104	5,378	-2,304	-30
	Total	10,968	13,713	12,687	11,337	7,716	-3,252	-30
Pulp and paper	Direct	42,844	43,352	43,158	45,814	43,319	476	1
	Total	67,432	66,638	69,784	70,722	68,571	1,139	2
Solid, secondary	Direct	35,391	38,894	36,686	33,842	22,296	-13,095	-37
	Total	51,985	60,063	61,381	55,827	37,226	-14,759	-28
Pulp and paper products	Direct	40,885	40,876	40,670	42,459	37,758	-3,126	-8
	Total	62,746	62,464	62,623	64,248	56,826	-5,920	-9
Total	Direct	168,896	174,470	167,013	164,084	128,896	-40,000	-24
	Total	250,703	260,291	255,663	249,270	200,556	-50,147	-20

Source: IMpact analysis for PLANning (IMPLAN) V3.0.

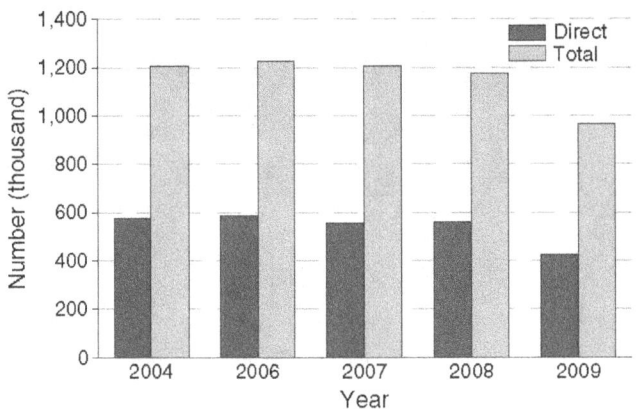

Figure 17—Forest sector employment (number of jobs) in the South by year and effect (direct and total).

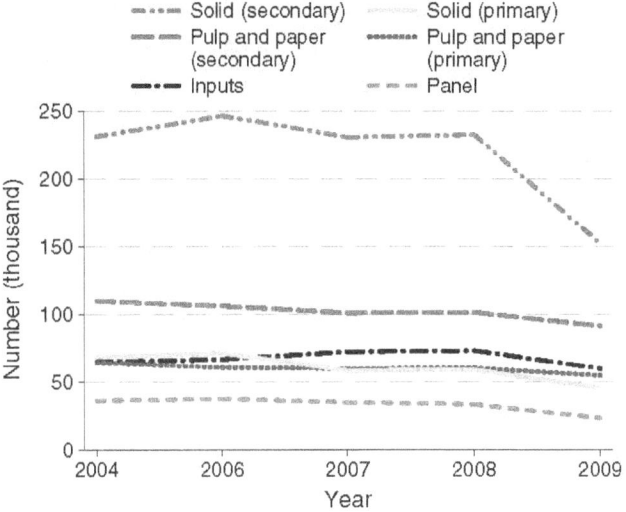

Figure 19—Forest sector direct impact effect on employment (number of jobs) by year and sector type, Southern Region.

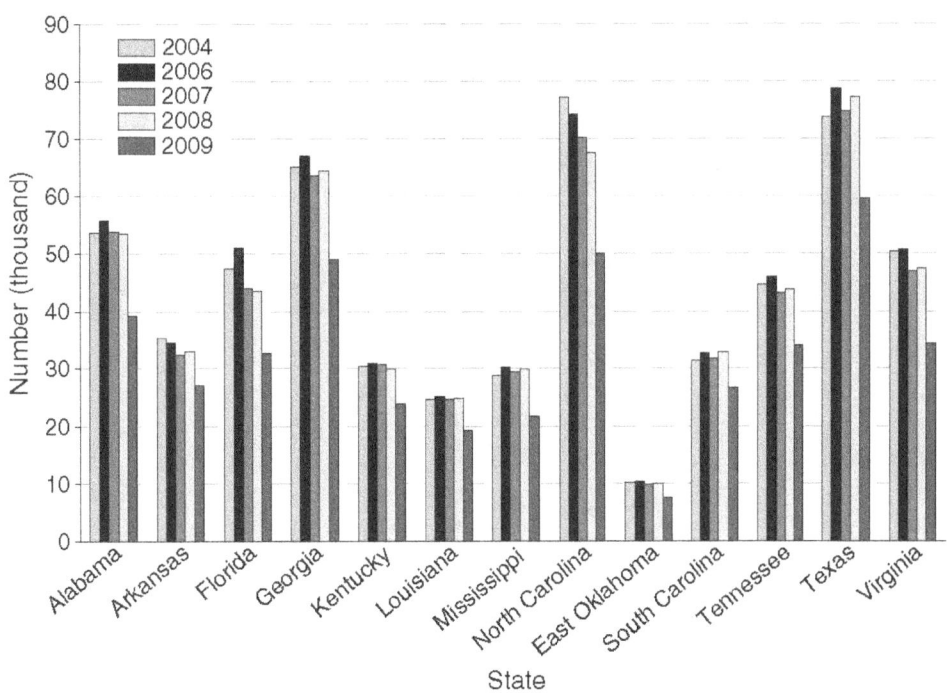

Figure 18—Forest sector direct impact effect on employment (number of jobs) by State and year.

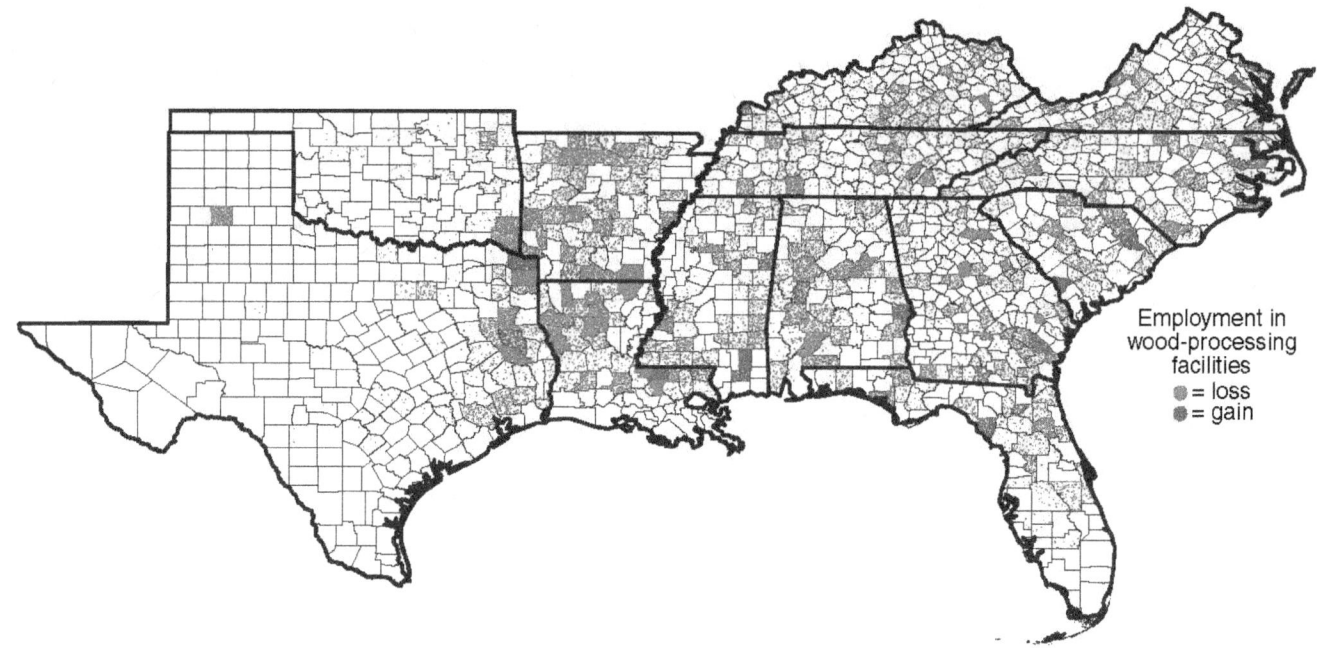

Figure 20—Total change in employment of primary wood-processing facilities as derived by timber product output survey, Southern United States, 2005–09. Each dot represents one individual.

Trends in the South's Timberland Area, Management, Growth, and Removals

Since 1985, timberland acreage across the Southern United States has remained relatively stable or has increased slightly with some loss of naturally regenerated acres concurrent with an increase in planted acres (fig. 21, with detailed tables by State in tables A.36–A.43). In 2010, the South's timberland acreage was at a historical high of 207.65 million acres, of which 77.6 percent were naturally regenerated acres and 22.4 percent planted acres. During this 1985 to 2010 period of stable timberland acreage, there was a decrease in the number of acres either partially or fully harvested for timber, and over time, this decrease has been steady (fig. 22). In 2010, 12 percent of the total timberland acres in the South

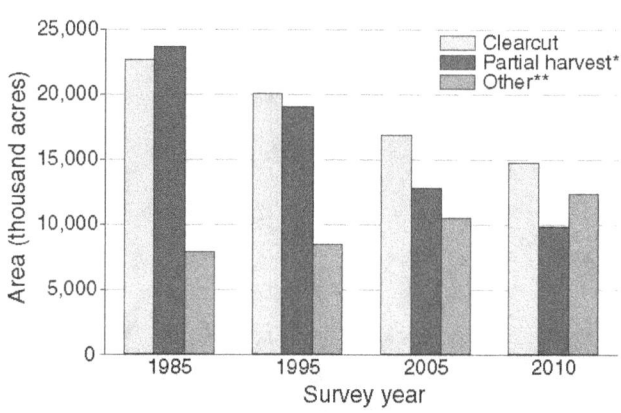

*Partial harvest combines both partial harvest and seed tree/shelterwood harvests.

**Other includes thinnings, timber stand improvement, salvage, firewood, precommercial thinning, as well as burning, herbicide, and other treatments.

Figure 22—Southwide timberland area by survey year and treatment type.

experienced some form of final harvesting. Conversely, the number of acres thinned or otherwise treated as part of timberland management has steadily increased, reaching 6 percent of the total timberland acres in 2010 (fig. 22).

We can speculate about what drives these trends. In the short term, timberland owners may be postponing final harvest until market conditions improve. Also, parcelization and fragmentation of timberland ownership has risen due to increased urbanization, estate disposal, and the recent divestiture and sale of former forest industry lands (roughly 40 million acres) to timber investment and management

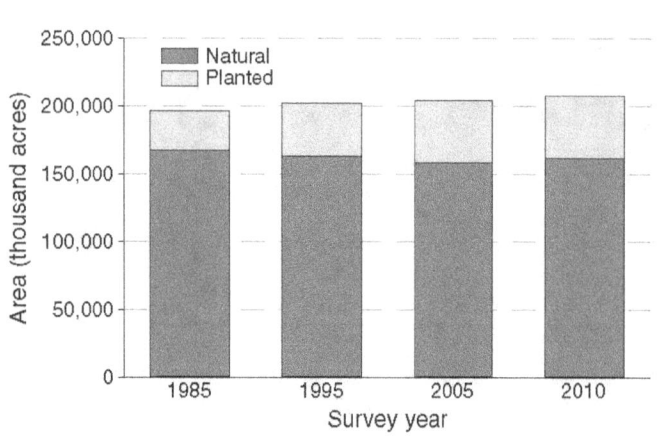

Figure 21—Southwide timberland area by survey year and stand origin.

organizations or real estate investment trusts. Timberlands are now a more liquid investment and more likely to be traded in the future, resulting in a decline in holding size. Smaller holding sizes may alter the operability of southern forests and change the desirability of holding forest assets, because traditional forest management activities are often difficult to perform on small tracts and are dissuaded in urban areas. Clearcuts, timber harvests, and other management activities, such as prescribed fire, may have been impacted and may continue to decline (Butler and Wear 2011).

We cannot fully attribute the reduction in harvested acres to the economic downturn that started in 2007, because the FIA data is an average of yearly estimates from both before and after 2007. Sharp deviations from the normal trend line, those that only occur for a few years or less, will be smoothed over by the averaging process. The degree to which we will be able to see whether the economic downturn, which began in 2007, will affect timberland harvests and removal will depend on how long those economic conditions last.

Volume growth on southern timberland has increased at a greater rate than timberland acreage (fig. 23, with detailed tables by State in tables A.31–A.34). This growth would indicate not only that Southern States are gaining wood volume from the increase in timberland acres but also that they are growing more wood on each timberland acre than in the past. The increase in timberland productivity could be attributed to the increase in acres planted with improved seedling stock and management practices, such as thinning for optimal tree growth. At the same time that volume growth has been increasing across the South, volume removals have held steady or decreased slightly (fig. 24), i.e., greater volumes per acre are being harvested from fewer

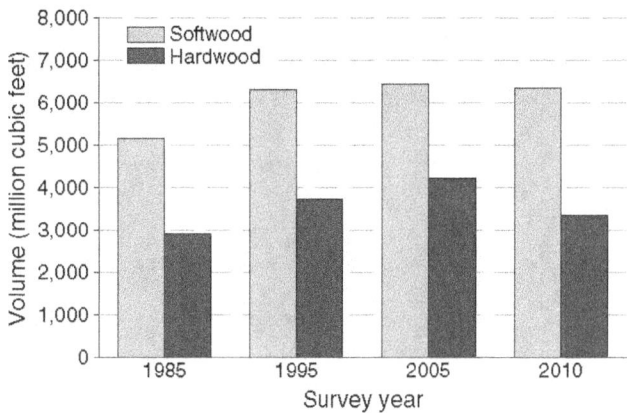

Figure 24—Average annual removals of all-live trees on southern timberlands by survey year and species group.

timberland acres, allowing the total harvested volume to remain relatively steady for softwoods. Hardwood removals, however, appear to have decreased from 2005 to 2010 (fig. 24). Seen side-by-side, annual volume growth on the South's timberland exceeds the annual volume removed, and for softwoods the degree to which growth exceeds removals has been increasing (figs. 25 and 26).

The combined effect of steady or increasing timberland acreage, fewer harvested acres, more acres actively managed for timber production, and stable to decreasing harvest volume has been a steady increase in both softwood and hardwood timber volumes on the South's timberlands (fig. 27). The trend of increasing timber volume has been relatively consistent across all Southern States (fig. 28).

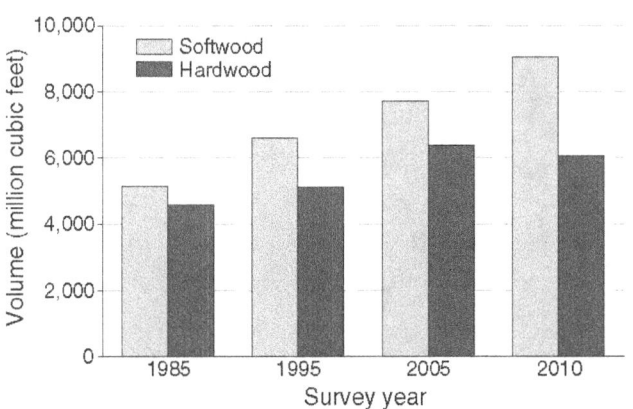

Figure 23—Average annual growth of all-live trees on southern timberlands by survey year and species group.

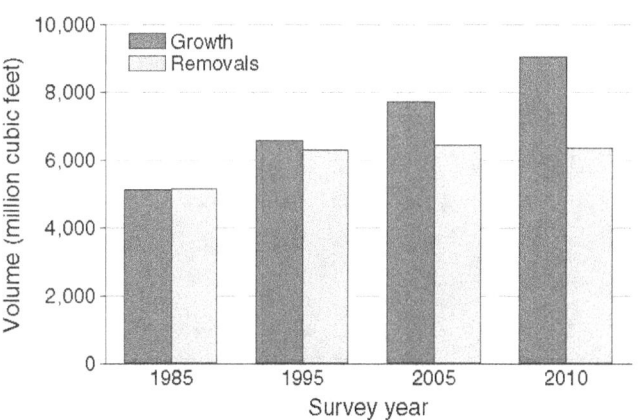

Figure 25—Average annual growth and removals of all-live softwood trees on southern timberlands by survey year.

17

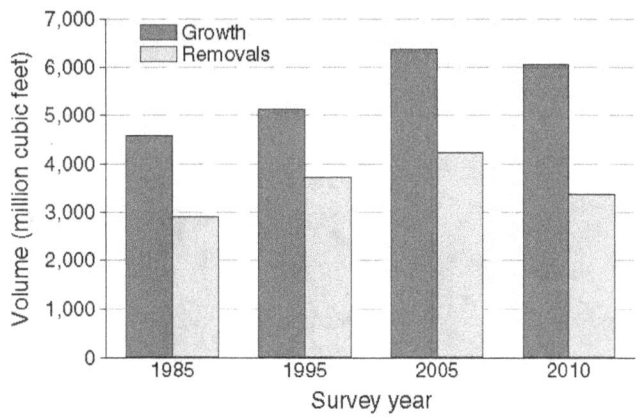

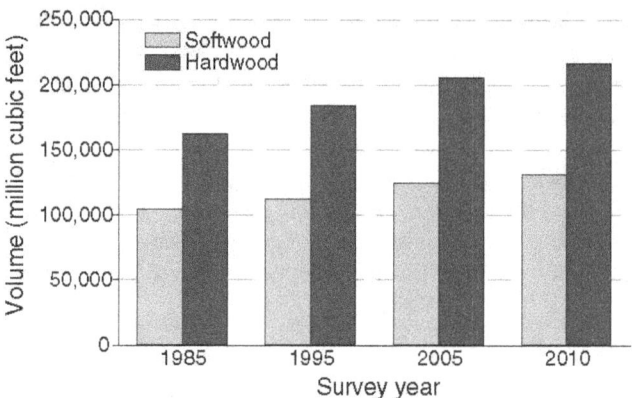

Figure 26—Average annual growth and removals of all-live hardwood trees on southern timberlands by survey year.

Figure 27—Volume of all-live trees on southern timberlands by survey year and species group.

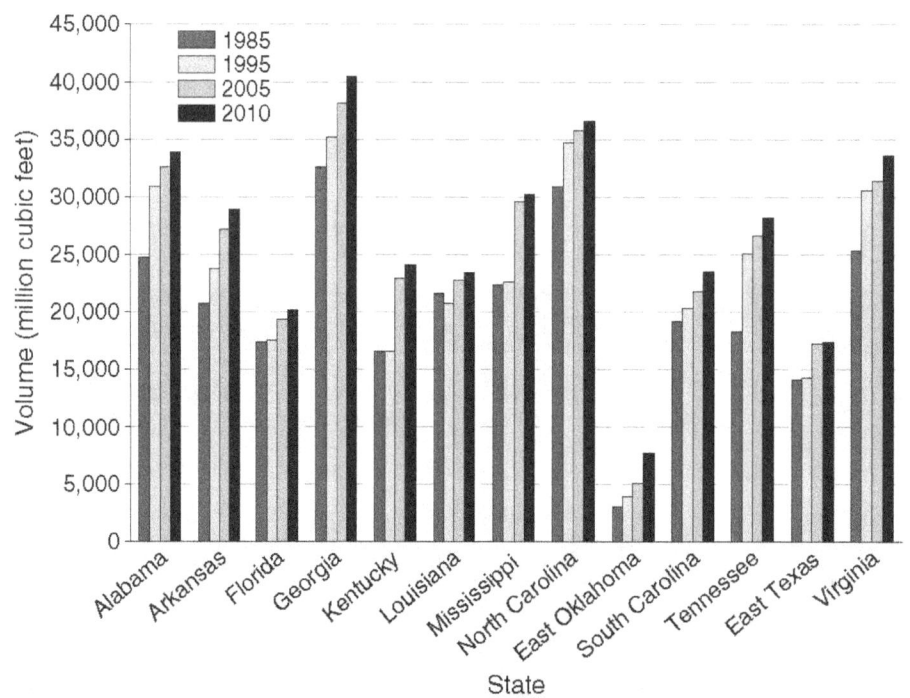

Figure 28—Volume of all-live hardwood and softwood trees on southern timberlands by State and survey year.

Summary

This report reviews how recent (2005-present) economic conditions have accelerated and accentuated mill closings and job losses, and, to a lesser extent, influenced forest management in the Southern United States. The number of primary roundwood-using mills has decreased steadily across the South since the 1970s. At the same time, mill output has increased steadily as the production of the remaining mills has increased. There has been a consolidation of productive capacity in the forest industry as mill size and output has increased. In recent years, with economic conditions unfavorable and mill output decreasing, mill closings have been on the rise. Particularly hard hit have been sawmills, largely due to the precipitous decline in housing starts and the loss of demand for southern pine structural timber. The North American engineered wood composite panel industry—after enjoying extended growth from the mid-1990s through 2005—likewise has been having a hard time, with wide-scale mill curtailments, closings, and consolidations. There are significant job losses from mill closings but the ripple effect goes beyond that. Other businesses that relied on the mill's business are affected, as are other businesses in the community that depended on the spending power of the mill workers.

There are indications that recent economic conditions are affecting the South's timberland management but the short term impacts are less marked. This may be for two reasons. First, the observed trends are a continuation of longer term patterns. Second, the FIA data used have a built-in timelag in the collection and reporting of data about forests, with the result that current realities and events might not match the available data. For many years, reports have shown stable or increasing timberland and wood volumes across the South. Reports have shown a decrease in the number of acres harvested but an increase in the removed volume from those decreasing acres, a finding that indicates that greater volumes are now harvested from an acre of land than in the past. Although the harvested acreage is decreasing, treated acreage concurrently is increasing, a trend that indicates that landowners are postponing final harvest, perhaps in anticipation of improved market conditions while investing in management activities that maintain and increase the value of their timberlands. If these land management practices continue, the result will be an abundance of mature stands consisting of larger-diameter trees across the region and relatively fewer younger, more recently regenerated stands.

For Additional Information

The FIA program makes the data it collects publically available in summary publications, online data query tools, and direct assistance to those looking for information on the status and trends of the South's forests and forest industry. Much of the historical information presented in this report can also be found in the numerous State and regional-level TPO and FIA reports produced by the Forest Service, Southern Research Station's FIA program. These reports and other publications related to the FIA program can be found and downloaded in electronic form using the online search engine found at the Web site http://www.srs.fs.usda.gov/pubs/.

The TPO database retrieval system helps customers answer questions about timber harvesting and use in the Southern Region. This system acts as an interface to a standard set of consistently coded TPO data for each State and county in the region and Nation. This regional and national set of TPO data consists of 11 variables that describe for each county the roundwood products harvested, logging residues left in the woods, other timber removals (i.e., land clearing and reserved timber removals), and wood and bark residues generated by the county's primary wood-using mills. The system is available through the FIA Web site http://srsfia2.fs.fed.us/.

Links to the online tools to access the FIADB are also available at the FIA Web site listed above or directly at http://www.fia.fs.fed.us/tools-data/default.asp. These tools allow users to query the FIA data in a wide variety of ways and to produce customized tables and mapped representations of those data. The Web site also has links to the FIA DataMart where users can directly download data, links to training and tutorials on how to use the FIADB and tools, and contact information for questions or assistance from each of the regional FIA offices.

Acknowledgments

The Southern Research Station gratefully acknowledges the cooperation and assistance provided by all of the State forestry agencies and the cooperative extension services in collecting mill and plot data, and to forest industry and mill managers for providing timber product information. Special appreciation to Tony Johnson, recently retired from the Southern Research Station's FIA unit, for his tireless efforts in compiling and maintaining historical TPO data throughout his career.

Literature Cited

Abt, K.L. 2011. Chapter 12. Employment and income trends and projections for forest-based sectors in the U.S. South. In: Southern forest futures project. Technical report. Research Triangle Park, NC: U.S. Department of Agriculture Forest Service, Forestry Sciences Laboratory. [Not paged]. Chartered by: U.S. Department of Agriculture Forest Service, Southern Research Station; Southern Region, Atlanta, GA. In cooperation with: Southern Group of State Foresters. http://www.srs.fs.usda.gov/futures/reports/draft/Frame.htm. [Date accessed: March 1, 2012].

Bechtold, W.A.; Patterson, P.L. Editors. 2005. The enhanced forest inventory and analysis program—national sampling design and estimation procedures. Gen. Tech. Rep. SRS–80. Asheville, NC: U.S. Department of Agriculture Forest Service, Southern Research Station. 85 p.

Bentley, J.W. 2003. The South's timber industry—an assessment of timber product output and use, 1999. Resour. Bull. SRS–85. Asheville, NC: U.S. Department of Agriculture Forest Service, Southern Research Station. 71 p.

Butler, B.J.; Wear, D.N. 2011. Chapter 6. Forest ownership dynamics of southern forests. In: Southern forest futures project. Technical report. Research Triangle Park, NC: U.S. Department of Agriculture Forest Service, Forestry Sciences Laboratory. [Not paged]. Chartered by: U.S. Department of Agriculture Forest Service, Southern Research Station; Southern Region, Atlanta, GA. In cooperation with: Southern Group of State Foresters. http://www.srs.fs.usda.gov/futures/reports/draft/Frame.htm. [Date accessed: March 1, 2012].

Food and Agriculture Organization. 2011. State of the World's Forests 2011. Rome, Italy: Food and Agriculture Organization of the United Nations. 164 p. http://www.fao.org/docrep/013/i2000e/i2000e00.htm. [Date accessed unknown].

Johnson, T.G.; Bentley, J.W.; Howell, M. 2006. The South's timber industry—an assessment of timber product output and use, 2003. Resour. Bull. SRS–114. Asheville, NC: U.S. Department of Agriculture Forest Service, Southern Research Station. 52 p.

Johnson, T.G.; Bentley, J.W.; Howell, M. 2008a. Historical trends of timber product output in the South. Resour. Bull. SRS–138. Asheville, NC: U.S. Department of Agriculture Forest Service, Southern Research Station. 70 p.

Johnson, T.G.; Bentley, J.W.; Howell, M. 2008b. The South's timber industry—an assessment of timber product output and use, 2005. Resour. Bull. SRS–135. Asheville, NC: U.S. Department of Agriculture Forest Service, Southern Research Station. 52 p.

Johnson, T.G.; Bentley, J.W.; Howell, M. 2009. The South's timber industry—an assessment of timber product output and use, 2007. Resour. Bull. SRS–164. Asheville, NC: U.S. Department of Agriculture Forest Service, Southern Research Station. 52 p.

Johnson, T.G.; Bentley, J.W.; Howell, M. 2011. The South's timber industry—an assessment of timber product output and use, 2009. Resour. Bull. SRS–182. Asheville, NC: U.S. Department of Agriculture Forest Service, Southern Research Station. 44 p.

Minnesota IMPLAN Group, Inc. 2009. IMPLAN System (data and software). Hudson, WI: Minnesota IMPLAN Group, Inc. www.implan.com. [Date accessed unknown].

Scott, C.T.; Bechtold, W.A.; Reams, G.A. [and others]. 2005. Sample-based estimators used by the forest inventory and analysis national information management system. In: Bechtold, W.A.; Patterson, P.L. Editors. The enhanced forest inventory and analysis program—national sampling design and estimation procedures. Gen. Tech. Rep. SRS–80. Asheville, NC: U.S. Department of Agriculture Forest Service, Southern Research Station: 43–67.

Smith, W.B. tech. coord.; Miles, P.D., data coord.; Perry, C.H., map coord.; Pugh, S.A., data CD coord. 2009. Forest resources of the United States, 2007. Gen. Tech. Rep. WO–78. Washington, DC: U.S. Department of Agriculture Forest Service, Washington Office. 336 p.

Woudenberg, S.W.; Conkling, B.L.; O'Connell, B.M. [and others]. 2010. The forest inventory and analysis database: database description and users manual version 4.0 for phase 2. Gen. Tech. Rep. RMRS–GTR–245. Fort Collins, CO: U.S. Department of Agriculture Forest Service, Rocky Mountain Research Station. 336 p.

Appendix

List of Tables

Table A.37—Area of timberland by State, survey year, stand origin, and stand treatment, 1990s periodic inventories

Table A.38—Area of timberland by State, survey year, stand origin, and stand treatment, 2005 moving average inventory

Table A.39—Area of timberland by State, survey year, stand origin, and stand treatment, 2010 moving average inventory

Table A.40—Current volume, average annual growth, average annual removals, and average annual saw-log removals of all-live trees by State and survey year, 1980s periodic inventories

Table A.41—Current volume, average annual growth, average annual removals, and average annual saw-log removals of all-live trees by State and survey year, 1990s periodic inventories

Table A.42—Current volume, average annual growth, average annual removals, and average annual saw-log removals of all-live trees by State and survey year, 2005 moving average inventory

Table A.43—Current volume, average annual growth, average annual removals, and average annual saw-log removals of all-live trees by State and survey year, 2010 moving average inventory

Table A.1—Industrial roundwood output, by year of survey, species group, and product, Alabama

State, year, and species group	All products	Saw logs	Veneer logs	Composite board	Pulpwood	Other industrial[a]
			thousand cubic feet			
Alabama, 1951						
Softwood	345,863	210,934	12,041	0	104,970	17,918
Hardwood	131,423	99,941	15,249	0	1,091	15,142
Total	477,286	310,875	27,290	0	106,061	33,060
Alabama, 1962						
Softwood	303,279	122,948	1,434	0	163,940	14,957
Hardwood	122,913	50,756	14,509	0	51,590	6,058
Total	426,192	173,704	15,943	0	215,530	21,015
Alabama, 1971						
Softwood	525,613	195,343	35,719	0	277,825	16,726
Hardwood	192,522	66,418	9,568	0	114,301	2,235
Total	718,135	261,761	45,287	0	392,126	18,961
Alabama, 1982						
Softwood	611,087	215,634	75,097	0	309,453	10,903
Hardwood	227,571	67,809	10,667	0	148,243	852
Total	838,658	283,443	85,764	0	457,696	11,755
Alabama, 1985						
Softwood	620,829	240,808	74,621	0	293,614	11,786
Hardwood	290,205	72,403	9,477	0	207,262	1,063
Total	911,034	313,211	84,098	0	500,876	12,849
Alabama, 1989						
Softwood	669,914	296,307	110,191	0	254,234	9,182
Hardwood	329,005	75,903	12,970	0	240,117	15
Total	998,919	372,210	123,161	0	494,351	9,197
Alabama, 1995[b c]						
Softwood	924,226	399,291	74,873	0	415,503	34,559
Hardwood	375,523	73,509	19,559	0	281,998	457
Total	1,299,749	472,800	94,432	0	697,501	35,016
Alabama, 1997[c]						
Softwood	956,765	382,123	74,921	13,562	462,596	23,563
Hardwood	388,547	68,003	17,887	289	302,310	58
Total	1,345,312	450,126	92,808	13,851	764,906	23,621
Alabama, 1999[c]						
Softwood	890,931	353,832	85,120	12,484	417,631	21,864
Hardwood	319,211	71,945	23,903	267	223,048	48
Total	1,210,142	425,777	109,023	12,751	640,679	21,912
Alabama, 2003[c]						
Softwood	806,084	335,571	84,767	22,863	342,360	20,523
Hardwood	271,516	69,046	22,595	1,138	178,737	0
Total	1,077,600	404,617	107,362	24,001	521,097	20,523

continued

25

Table A.1—Industrial roundwood output, by year of survey, species group, and product, Alabama (continued)

State, year, and species group	All products	Saw logs	Veneer logs	Composite board	Pulpwood	Other industrial[a]
	thousand cubic feet					
Alabama, 2005[c]						
Softwood	878,708	371,660	74,444	43,760	372,736	16,108
Hardwood	264,075	53,636	18,824	1,509	190,046	60
Total	1,142,783	425,296	93,268	45,269	562,782	16,168
Alabama, 2007						
Softwood	828,095	354,977	60,069	27,777	374,966	10,306
Hardwood	273,971	58,030	15,100	1,610	199,131	100
Total	1,102,066	413,007	75,169	29,387	574,097	10,406
Alabama, 2009						
Softwood	597,013	187,930	21,166	0	360,279	27,638
Hardwood	206,304	40,352	7,861	0	154,809	3,282
Total	803,317	228,282	29,027	0	515,088	30,920

[a] Includes poles, pilings, posts, and other miscellaneous products.

[b] Composite board volume was included with other industrial.

[c] Pulpwood includes roundwood chipped.

Table A.2—Industrial roundwood output, by year of survey, species group, and product, Arkansas

State, year, and species group	All products	Saw logs	Veneer logs	Composite board	Pulpwood	Other industrial[a]
			thousand cubic feet			
Arkansas, 1948						
Softwood	204,909	152,129	0	0	42,749	10,031
Hardwood	117,267	79,835	16,504	0	3,872	17,056
Total	322,176	231,964	16,504	0	46,621	27,087
Arkansas, 1958						
Softwood	187,842	109,297	0	0	67,016	11,529
Hardwood	89,370	62,321	7,385	0	11,537	8,127
Total	277,212	171,618	7,385	0	78,553	19,656
Arkansas, 1968						
Softwood	258,781	129,889	33,920	0	81,963	13,009
Hardwood	131,672	74,828	3,392	0	41,620	11,832
Total	390,453	204,717	37,312	0	123,583	24,841
Arkansas, 1971						
Softwood	309,082	151,280	39,862	0	100,130	17,810
Hardwood	141,388	70,301	2,728	0	51,871	16,488
Total	450,470	221,581	42,590	0	152,001	34,298
Arkansas, 1977						
Softwood	381,470	205,286	47,195	0	117,823	11,166
Hardwood	135,406	69,502	1,414	0	61,247	3,243
Total	516,876	274,788	48,609	0	179,070	14,409
Arkansas, 1987						
Softwood	385,266	207,000	82,000	0	93,474	2,792
Hardwood	153,577	75,000	2,000	0	73,327	3,250
Total	538,843	282,000	84,000	0	166,801	6,042
Arkansas, 1996[b]						
Softwood	423,524	225,807	68,257	50	125,131	4,279
Hardwood	212,554	88,965	6,047	187	117,344	11
Total	636,078	314,772	74,304	237	242,475	4,290
Arkansas, 1999[b]						
Softwood	495,132	231,530	77,621	437	182,819	2,725
Hardwood	196,614	88,325	5,927	188	102,146	28
Total	691,746	319,855	83,548	625	284,965	2,753
Arkansas, 2002[b]						
Softwood	506,629	252,493	89,633	27,141	134,317	3,045
Hardwood	172,985	89,622	4,859	187	78,276	41
Total	679,614	342,115	94,492	27,328	212,593	3,086
Arkansas, 2005[b]						
Softwood	538,653	289,161	89,449	27,475	130,774	1,794
Hardwood	210,185	100,433	5,717	187	103,848	0
Total	748,838	389,594	95,166	27,662	234,622	1,794

continued

Table A.2—Industrial roundwood output, by year of survey, species group, and product, Arkansas (continued)

State, year, and species group	All products	Saw logs	Veneer logs	Composite board	Pulpwood	Other industrial[a]
			thousand cubic feet			
Arkansas, 2007						
Softwood	474,713	257,812	56,095	24,760	135,715	331
Hardwood	195,046	95,700	5,283	0	94,061	2
Total	669,759	353,512	61,378	24,760	229,776	333
Arkansas, 2009						
Softwood	361,741	169,755	43,333	14,260	133,200	1,193
Hardwood	127,692	45,456	951	0	81,285	0
Total	489,433	215,211	44,284	14,260	214,485	1,193

[a] Includes poles, pilings, posts, and other miscellaneous products.

[b] Pulpwood includes roundwood chipped.

Table A.3—Industrial roundwood output, by year of survey, species group, and product, Florida

State, year, and species group	All products	Saw logs	Veneer logs	Composite board	Pulpwood	Other industrial[a]
	thousand cubic feet					
Florida, 1948						
Softwood	200,310	91,872	4,079	0	96,865	7,494
Hardwood	17,750	5,998	11,151	0	95	506
Total	218,060	97,870	15,230	0	96,960	8,000
Florida, 1958						
Softwood	185,394	42,635	98	0	134,245	8,416
Hardwood	19,826	6,952	6,485	0	4,885	1,504
Total	205,220	49,587	6,583	0	139,130	9,920
Florida, 1960						
Softwood	180,107	41,092	212	0	130,685	8,118
Hardwood	30,384	9,089	10,118	0	7,312	3,865
Total	210,491	50,181	10,330	0	137,997	11,983
Florida, 1969						
Softwood	254,919	43,791	4,815	0	200,528	5,785
Hardwood	39,261	9,363	10,842	0	18,227	829
Total	294,180	53,154	15,657	0	218,755	6,614
Florida, 1971						
Softwood	265,976	52,298	12,607	0	194,063	7,008
Hardwood	39,174	11,525	12,409	0	15,240	0
Total	305,150	63,823	25,016	0	209,303	7,008
Florida, 1973						
Softwood	280,873	63,149	8,785	0	202,863	6,076
Hardwood	31,624	6,353	9,880	0	15,391	0
Total	312,497	69,502	18,665	0	218,254	6,076
Florida, 1975						
Softwood	231,277	56,956	1,849	0	169,131	3,341
Hardwood	25,606	6,713	4,362	0	14,531	0
Total	256,883	63,669	6,211	0	183,662	3,341
Florida, 1977[b]						
Softwood	290,480	74,421	7,910	0	204,669	3,480
Hardwood	33,078	5,895	3,183	0	24,000	0
Total	323,558	80,316	11,093	0	228,669	3,480
Florida, 1979[b]						
Softwood	371,791	124,671	12,055	0	227,903	7,162
Hardwood	42,094	9,625	3,749	0	28,720	0
Total	413,885	134,296	15,804	0	256,623	7,162
Florida, 1981[b]						
Softwood	378,128	107,611	15,180	0	246,259	9,078
Hardwood	38,514	6,866	2,855	0	28,793	0
Total	416,642	114,477	18,035	0	275,052	9,078

continued

Table A.3—Industrial roundwood output, by year of survey, species group, and product, Florida (continued)

State, year, and species group	All products	Saw logs	Veneer logs	Composite board	Pulpwood	Other industrial[a]
	thousand cubic feet					
Florida, 1983[b]						
Softwood	424,175	138,914	21,990	0	251,211	12,060
Hardwood	37,419	5,012	2,722	0	28,640	1,045
Total	461,594	143,926	24,712	0	279,851	13,105
Florida, 1984[b]						
Softwood	410,118	133,402	26,548	0	240,224	9,944
Hardwood	31,736	5,320	4,735	0	21,681	0
Total	441,854	138,722	31,283	0	261,905	9,944
Florida, 1985[b]						
Softwood	389,091	133,779	26,153	0	215,584	13,575
Hardwood	31,978	10,123	3,302	0	18,553	0
Total	421,069	143,902	29,455	0	234,137	13,575
Florida, 1986[b]						
Softwood	415,117	140,299	24,555	0	236,560	13,703
Hardwood	28,729	9,643	1,538	0	17,440	108
Total	443,846	149,942	26,093	0	254,000	13,811
Florida, 1987[b]						
Softwood	453,543	139,079	27,734	0	267,032	19,698
Hardwood	26,415	3,205	1,450	0	21,438	322
Total	479,958	142,284	29,184	0	288,470	20,020
Florida, 1989[b]						
Softwood	450,095	137,978	19,868	291	270,713	21,245
Hardwood	32,603	3,653	1,763	776	25,600	811
Total	482,698	141,631	21,631	1,067	296,313	22,056
Florida, 1991[b]						
Softwood	496,877	153,825	19,698	291	298,454	24,609
Hardwood	36,035	2,312	1,616	776	30,936	395
Total	532,912	156,137	21,314	1,067	329,390	25,004
Florida, 1993[b]						
Softwood	468,049	148,044	28,478	360	262,372	28,795
Hardwood	50,225	4,365	1,559	2,581	41,384	336
Total	518,274	152,409	30,037	2,941	303,756	29,131
Florida, 1995[b]						
Softwood	475,817	146,856	24,347	0	280,917	23,697
Hardwood	51,217	6,078	1,802	3,012	40,094	231
Total	527,034	152,934	26,149	3,012	321,011	23,928
Florida, 1997[b]						
Softwood	467,597	156,779	28,279	0	251,618	30,921
Hardwood	49,758	5,075	1,559	6,403	35,883	838
Total	517,355	161,854	29,838	6,403	287,501	31,759

continued

Table A.3—Industrial roundwood output, by year of survey, species group, and product, Florida (continued)

State, year, and species group	All products	Saw logs	Veneer logs	Composite board	Pulpwood	Other industrial[a]
				thousand cubic feet		
Florida, 1999[b]						
Softwood	445,749	162,959	32,770	0	222,119	27,901
Hardwood	52,813	4,382	1,211	7,380	39,202	638
Total	498,562	167,341	33,981	7,380	261,321	28,539
Florida, 2003[b]						
Softwood	468,577	166,217	30,492	1,326	243,796	26,746
Hardwood	40,109	4,454	1,437	6,400	26,939	879
Total	508,686	170,671	31,929	7,726	270,735	27,625
Florida, 2005[b]						
Softwood	416,796	162,617	24,905	14,164	193,390	21,720
Hardwood	28,349	4,415	1,526	1,418	20,111	879
Total	445,145	167,032	26,431	15,582	213,501	22,599
Florida, 2007						
Softwood	468,374	173,532	24,229	28,335	221,021	21,257
Hardwood	22,687	3,899	1,371	1,218	15,533	666
Total	491,061	177,431	25,600	29,553	236,554	21,923
Florida, 2009						
Softwood	454,527	117,773	18,686	25,104	249,195	43,769
Hardwood	20,051	1,864	1,256	236	16,029	666
Total	474,578	119,637	19,942	25,340	265,224	44,435

[a] Includes poles, pilings, posts, and other miscellaneous products.

[b] Pulpwood includes roundwood chipped.

Table A.4—Industrial roundwood output, by year of survey, species group, and product, Georgia

State, year, and species group	All products	Saw logs	Veneer logs	Composite board	Pulpwood	Other industrial[a]
				thousand cubic feet		
Georgia, 1937						
Softwood	195,149	163,859	6,543	0	15,317	9,430
Hardwood	51,941	33,641	13,697	0	713	3,890
Total	247,090	197,500	20,240	0	16,030	13,320
Georgia, 1952						
Softwood	505,355	311,544	821	0	168,707	24,283
Hardwood	116,533	76,503	22,379	0	7,824	9,827
Total	621,888	388,047	23,200	0	176,531	34,110
Georgia, 1961						
Softwood	450,673	174,594	66	0	265,844	10,169
Hardwood	98,167	41,804	17,922	0	36,683	1,758
Total	548,840	216,398	17,988	0	302,527	11,927
Georgia, 1971						
Softwood	682,548	239,229	27,147	0	398,001	18,171
Hardwood	119,258	57,502	13,200	0	46,966	1,590
Total	801,806	296,731	40,347	0	444,967	19,761
Georgia, 1974						
Softwood	712,644	236,560	28,765	0	430,584	16,735
Hardwood	139,025	67,201	15,295	0	56,077	452
Total	851,669	303,761	44,060	0	486,661	17,187
Georgia, 1977						
Softwood	762,393	322,462	44,162	0	382,352	13,417
Hardwood	130,060	61,859	15,566	0	52,635	0
Total	892,453	384,321	59,728	0	434,987	13,417
Georgia, 1980[b]						
Softwood	860,129	354,591	37,938	0	455,480	12,120
Hardwood	133,098	71,653	11,303	0	50,142	0
Total	993,227	426,244	49,241	0	505,622	12,120
Georgia, 1983[b c]						
Softwood	960,879	406,922	63,864	0	468,569	21,524
Hardwood	150,869	65,619	13,393	0	71,857	0
Total	1,111,748	472,541	77,257	0	540,426	21,524
Georgia, 1986[b c]						
Softwood	1,015,435	443,204	64,093	0	490,845	17,293
Hardwood	187,149	75,338	14,296	0	97,515	0
Total	1,202,584	518,542	78,389	0	588,360	17,293
Georgia, 1989[b]						
Softwood	920,175	408,489	69,077	19,672	407,876	15,061
Hardwood	193,419	65,678	12,863	6,880	107,987	11
Total	1,113,594	474,167	81,940	26,552	515,863	15,072

continued

Table A.4—Industrial roundwood output, by year of survey, species group, and product, Georgia (continued)

State, year, and species group	All products	Saw logs	Veneer logs	Composite board	Pulpwood	Other industrial[a]
	thousand cubic feet					
Georgia, 1992[b]						
Softwood	1,022,308	444,044	54,849	38,360	427,816	57,239
Hardwood	207,613	62,341	17,756	6,588	120,039	889
Total	1,229,921	506,385	72,605	44,948	547,855	58,128
Georgia, 1995[b]						
Softwood	1,020,506	486,848	58,924	36,900	422,807	15,027
Hardwood	291,001	65,361	20,367	10,343	194,458	472
Total	1,311,507	552,209	79,291	47,243	617,265	15,499
Georgia, 1997[b]						
Softwood	1,000,897	442,584	61,469	42,653	437,957	16,234
Hardwood	279,684	77,028	15,649	7,134	179,336	537
Total	1,280,581	519,612	77,118	49,787	617,293	16,771
Georgia, 1999[b]						
Softwood	997,446	446,881	59,547	39,996	431,017	20,005
Hardwood	247,095	61,768	15,858	6,176	162,535	758
Total	1,244,541	508,649	75,405	46,172	593,552	20,763
Georgia, 2001[b]						
Softwood	906,092	424,068	58,370	41,813	365,687	16,154
Hardwood	216,569	61,063	14,541	4,960	135,292	713
Total	1,122,661	485,131	72,911	46,773	500,979	16,867
Georgia, 2003[b]						
Softwood	961,947	375,705	56,986	45,373	457,619	26,264
Hardwood	190,907	65,442	11,488	2,365	111,277	335
Total	1,152,854	441,147	68,474	47,738	568,896	26,599
Georgia, 2005[b]						
Softwood	999,395	394,723	66,742	56,350	455,654	25,926
Hardwood	165,876	63,480	7,660	6,658	87,174	904
Total	1,165,271	458,203	74,402	63,008	542,828	26,830
Georgia, 2007						
Softwood	1,038,307	352,142	57,684	95,415	507,960	25,106
Hardwood	171,509	59,543	5,804	2,786	102,767	609
Total	1,209,816	411,685	63,488	98,201	610,727	25,715
Georgia, 2009						
Softwood	908,567	266,169	42,145	57,522	503,176	39,555
Hardwood	144,120	43,310	3,279	370	94,244	2,917
Total	1,052,687	309,479	45,424	57,892	597,420	42,472

[a] Includes poles, pilings, posts, and other miscellaneous products.

[b] Pulpwood includes roundwood chipped.

[c] Composite board volume was included with other industrial for 1983 and 1986.

Table A.5—Industrial roundwood output, by year of survey, species group, and product, Kentucky

State, year, and species group	All products	Saw logs	Veneer logs	Composite board	Pulpwood	Other industrial[a]
	thousand cubic feet					
Kentucky, 1948						
Softwood	10,100	7,100	0	0	0	3,000
Hardwood	102,115	80,746	7,452	0	3,366	10,551
Total	112,215	87,846	7,452	0	3,366	13,551
Kentucky, 1962						
Softwood	9,198	4,651	0	0	2,594	1,953
Hardwood	81,325	67,708	4,901	0	3,129	5,587
Total	90,523	72,359	4,901	0	5,723	7,540
Kentucky, 1969						
Softwood	10,100	6,700	0	0	2,200	1,200
Hardwood	86,800	71,600	4,000	0	4,500	6,700
Total	96,900	78,300	4,000	0	6,700	7,900
Kentucky, 1974						
Softwood	10,106	6,199	0	0	2,108	1,799
Hardwood	87,961	71,481	2,586	0	9,205	4,689
Total	98,067	77,680	2,586	0	11,313	6,488
Kentucky, 1986						
Softwood	12,007	7,258	14	0	2,181	2,554
Hardwood	125,588	109,380	1,930	0	12,148	2,130
Total	137,595	116,638	1,944	0	14,329	4,684
Kentucky, 1995[b]						
Softwood	11,156	6,015	0	0	3,336	1,805
Hardwood	175,030	155,225	1,009	0	17,034	1,762
Total	186,186	161,240	1,009	0	20,370	3,567
Kentucky, 1997[b]						
Softwood	10,416	5,668	126	602	2,359	1,661
Hardwood	184,189	155,297	4,954	9,228	14,502	208
Total	194,605	160,965	5,080	9,830	16,861	1,869
Kentucky, 1999[b]						
Softwood	10,680	5,855	88	1,894	2,162	681
Hardwood	209,238	173,019	7,472	9,994	17,322	1,431
Total	219,918	178,874	7,560	11,888	19,484	2,112
Kentucky, 2001[b]						
Softwood	9,675	5,942	88	1,421	1,074	1,150
Hardwood	185,950	149,754	8,529	10,215	16,022	1,430
Total	195,625	155,696	8,617	11,636	17,096	2,580
Kentucky, 2003[b]						
Softwood	10,444	4,642	88	981	3,143	1,590
Hardwood	176,140	141,027	5,310	11,519	18,240	44
Total	186,584	145,669	5,398	12,500	21,383	1,634

continued

Table A.5—Industrial roundwood output, by year of survey, species group, and product, Kentucky, (continued)

State, year, and species group	All products	Saw logs	Veneer logs	Composite board	Pulpwood	Other industrial[a]
			thousand cubic feet			
Kentucky, 2005[b]						
Softwood	12,536	4,429	268	2,038	4,162	1,639
Hardwood	178,644	138,870	7,280	12,061	20,389	44
Total	191,180	143,299	7,548	14,099	24,551	1,683
Kentucky, 2007						
Softwood	11,538	4,164	7	1,929	4,187	1,251
Hardwood	174,158	140,254	6,538	6,946	20,420	0
Total	185,696	144,418	6,545	8,875	24,607	1,251
Kentucky, 2009						
Softwood	9,877	2,754	3	0	5,788	1,332
Hardwood	126,461	99,861	3,369	0	22,139	1,092
Total	136,338	102,615	3,372	0	27,927	2,424

[a] Includes poles, pilings, posts, and other miscellaneous products.

[b] Pulpwood includes roundwood chipped.

Table A.6—Industrial roundwood output, by year of survey, species group, and product, Louisiana

State, year, and species group	All products	Saw logs	Veneer logs	Composite board	Pulpwood	Other industrial[a]
	thousand cubic feet					
Louisiana, 1937						
Softwood	214,650	173,720	910	0	29,740	10,280
Hardwood	142,750	113,900	21,590	0	310	6,950
Total	357,400	287,620	22,500	0	30,050	17,230
Louisiana, 1953						
Softwood	177,064	71,905	0	0	88,894	16,265
Hardwood	112,582	79,912	10,302	0	15,290	7,078
Total	289,646	151,817	10,302	0	104,184	23,343
Louisiana, 1962						
Softwood	221,154	97,930	0	0	111,452	11,772
Hardwood	99,213	57,445	4,982	0	32,551	4,235
Total	320,367	155,375	4,982	0	144,003	16,007
Louisiana, 1963						
Softwood	237,454	110,803	0	0	113,325	13,326
Hardwood	115,416	65,399	8,066	0	36,218	5,733
Total	352,870	176,202	8,066	0	149,543	19,059
Louisiana, 1973						
Softwood	437,934	123,340	96,245	0	199,526	18,823
Hardwood	123,214	58,427	2,608	0	61,377	802
Total	561,148	181,767	98,853	0	260,903	19,625
Louisiana, 1996[b]						
Softwood	505,539	153,800	122,240	0	223,263	6,236
Hardwood	121,686	27,631	896	0	91,278	1,881
Total	627,225	181,431	123,136	0	314,541	8,117
Louisiana, 1999[c]						
Softwood	648,345	229,859	147,777	22,751	246,672	1,286
Hardwood	153,889	39,201	695	11,557	102,436	0
Total	802,234	269,060	148,472	34,308	349,108	1,286
Louisiana, 2002[c]						
Softwood	589,691	230,394	136,832	23,863	191,096	7,506
Hardwood	130,645	42,609	641	12,176	75,219	0
Total	720,336	273,003	137,473	36,039	266,315	7,506
Louisiana, 2005[c]						
Softwood	710,637	282,659	144,915	26,248	254,488	2,327
Hardwood	154,897	60,402	695	11,730	82,070	0
Total	865,534	343,061	145,610	37,978	336,558	2,327

continued

Table A.6—Industrial roundwood output, by year of survey, species group, and product, Louisiana (continued)

State, year, and species group	All products	Saw logs	Veneer logs	Composite board	Pulpwood	Other industrial[a]
	thousand cubic feet					
Louisiana, 2007						
Softwood	683,898	264,861	130,054	19,046	266,738	3,199
Hardwood	130,555	50,766	463	109	79,217	0
Total	814,453	315,627	130,517	19,155	345,955	3,199
Louisiana, 2009						
Softwood	513,614	134,779	79,821	35,287	256,030	7,697
Hardwood	86,971	19,878	670	0	66,423	0
Total	600,585	154,657	80,491	35,287	322,453	7,697

[a] Includes poles, pilings, posts, and other miscellaneous products.

[b] Composite board volume was included with other industrial.

[c] Pulpwood includes roundwood chipped.

Table A.7—Industrial roundwood output, by year of survey, species group, and product, Mississippi

State, year, and species group	All products	Saw logs	Veneer logs	Composite board	Pulpwood	Other industrial[a]
	thousand cubic feet					
Mississippi, 1946						
Softwood	258,200	174,400	2,800	0	64,200	16,800
Hardwood	214,000	135,200	35,500	0	15,200	28,100
Total	472,200	309,600	38,300	0	79,400	44,900
Mississippi, 1956						
Softwood	198,467	97,320	0	0	89,343	11,804
Hardwood	179,451	84,252	15,239	0	68,468	11,492
Total	377,918	181,572	15,239	0	157,811	23,296
Mississippi, 1966						
Softwood	235,797	87,431	7,526	0	126,383	14,457
Hardwood	166,129	79,674	8,785	0	73,200	4,470
Total	401,926	167,105	16,311	0	199,583	18,927
Mississippi, 1972						
Softwood	383,111	117,523	56,175	0	191,773	17,640
Hardwood	176,200	72,056	5,234	0	94,234	4,676
Total	559,311	189,579	61,409	0	286,007	22,316
Mississippi, 1976						
Softwood	482,282	200,549	71,705	0	184,269	25,759
Hardwood	195,133	87,073	3,003	0	102,492	2,565
Total	677,415	287,622	74,708	0	286,761	28,324
Mississippi, 1995[b]						
Softwood	685,722	406,154	57,510	12,415	208,192	1,451
Hardwood	348,313	86,628	5,559	10,603	245,523	0
Total	1,034,035	492,782	63,069	23,018	453,715	1,451
Mississippi, 1999[b]						
Softwood	708,631	402,071	64,920	12,683	227,311	1,646
Hardwood	282,654	88,495	5,983	11,611	176,565	0
Total	991,285	490,566	70,903	24,294	403,876	1,646
Mississippi, 2002[b]						
Softwood	688,235	419,174	72,261	27,061	168,144	1,595
Hardwood	239,054	107,028	5,865	7,402	118,759	0
Total	927,289	526,202	78,126	34,463	286,903	1,595
Mississippi, 2005[b]						
Softwood	781,328	432,908	69,401	39,332	238,166	1,521
Hardwood	251,431	110,394	8,752	4,524	127,761	0
Total	1,032,759	543,302	78,153	43,856	365,927	1,521

continued

Table A.7—Industrial roundwood output, by year of survey, species group, and product, Mississippi (continued)

State, year, and species group	All products	Saw logs	Veneer logs	Composite board	Pulpwood	Other industrial[a]
	thousand cubic feet					
Mississippi, 2007						
Softwood	679,980	300,541	70,675	32,980	274,250	1,534
Hardwood	214,119	78,241	4,967	4,606	126,305	0
Total	894,099	378,782	75,642	37,586	400,555	1,534
Mississippi, 2009						
Softwood	529,421	165,049	44,484	17,969	298,486	3,433
Hardwood	155,618	54,541	2,420	526	97,936	195
Total	685,039	219,590	46,904	18,495	396,422	3,628

[a] Includes poles, pilings, posts, and other miscellaneous products.

[b] Pulpwood includes roundwood chipped.

Table A.8—Industrial roundwood output, by year of survey, species group, and product, North Carolina

State, year, and species group	All products	Saw logs	Veneer logs	Composite board	Pulpwood	Other industrial[a]
				thousand cubic feet		
North Carolina, 1955						
Softwood	309,789	204,665	3,654	0	88,000	13,470
Hardwood	108,760	54,703	19,118	0	22,848	12,091
Total	418,549	259,368	22,772	0	110,848	25,561
North Carolina, 1964						
Softwood	291,806	169,632	710	0	113,665	7,799
Hardwood	147,307	73,610	23,604	0	40,411	9,682
Total	439,113	243,242	24,314	0	154,076	17,481
North Carolina, 1967						
Softwood	323,820	169,383	10,365	0	127,939	16,133
Hardwood	154,597	73,900	22,786	0	54,113	3,798
Total	478,417	243,283	33,151	0	182,052	19,931
North Carolina, 1969						
Softwood	305,058	154,379	12,980	0	128,771	8,928
Hardwood	161,477	80,364	22,352	0	56,579	2,182
Total	466,535	234,743	35,332	0	185,350	11,110
North Carolina, 1973						
Softwood	373,522	178,126	49,799	0	143,698	1,899
Hardwood	202,303	89,940	17,629	0	92,243	2,491
Total	575,825	268,066	67,428	0	235,941	4,390
North Carolina, 1976[b]						
Softwood	360,528	178,489	31,643	0	148,968	1,428
Hardwood	162,349	72,559	11,262	0	78,195	333
Total	522,877	251,048	42,905	0	227,163	1,761
North Carolina, 1979[b]						
Softwood	345,590	175,692	34,496	0	134,625	777
Hardwood	188,745	85,717	9,644	0	89,494	3,890
Total	534,335	261,409	44,140	0	224,119	4,667
North Carolina, 1983[b]						
Softwood	368,098	177,685	35,964	0	153,318	1,131
Hardwood	219,120	98,017	14,506	0	101,056	5,541
Total	587,218	275,702	50,470	0	254,374	6,672
North Carolina, 1986[b c]						
Softwood	440,841	201,964	59,828	0	171,430	7,619
Hardwood	245,163	93,240	16,640	0	127,247	8,036
Total	686,004	295,204	76,468	0	298,677	15,655
North Carolina, 1987[b c]						
Softwood	472,488	215,719	48,892	0	194,421	13,456
Hardwood	274,627	115,382	19,402	0	126,115	13,728
Total	747,115	331,101	68,294	0	320,536	27,184

continued

Table A.8—Industrial roundwood output, by year of survey, species group, and product, North Carolina (continued)

State, year, and species group	All products	Saw logs	Veneer logs	Composite board	Pulpwood	Other industrial[a]
				thousand cubic feet		
North Carolina, 1990[b]						
Softwood	491,211	223,254	44,100	18,159	203,651	2,047
Hardwood	272,961	103,440	26,038	16,362	127,084	37
Total	764,172	326,694	70,138	34,521	330,735	2,084
North Carolina, 1992[b]						
Softwood	526,153	248,599	40,990	17,784	215,327	3,453
Hardwood	273,050	100,322	21,531	17,665	133,500	32
Total	799,203	348,921	62,521	35,449	348,827	3,485
North Carolina, 1994[b]						
Softwood	538,831	275,321	43,280	19,081	198,479	2,670
Hardwood	307,524	108,520	20,058	18,640	160,274	32
Total	846,355	383,841	63,338	37,721	358,753	2,702
North Carolina, 1995[b]						
Softwood	554,909	290,523	47,740	20,869	193,572	2,205
Hardwood	277,932	107,960	18,682	12,959	138,299	32
Total	832,841	398,483	66,422	33,828	331,871	2,237
North Carolina, 1997[b]						
Softwood	560,717	299,278	41,163	16,909	200,833	2,534
Hardwood	309,652	123,306	18,907	13,704	153,735	0
Total	870,369	422,584	60,070	30,613	354,568	2,534
North Carolina, 1999[b]						
Softwood	532,257	296,290	41,748	27,450	164,991	1,778
Hardwood	260,802	125,778	19,310	8,860	106,854	0
Total	793,059	422,068	61,058	36,310	271,845	1,778
North Carolina, 2001[b]						
Softwood	512,313	308,668	34,117	26,610	141,903	1,015
Hardwood	246,187	116,581	19,302	9,184	101,098	22
Total	758,500	425,249	53,419	35,794	243,001	1,037
North Carolina, 2003[b]						
Softwood	530,616	285,904	39,980	45,444	158,359	929
Hardwood	245,427	112,758	16,574	7,519	108,554	22
Total	776,043	398,662	56,554	52,963	266,913	951
North Carolina, 2005[b]						
Softwood	513,162	289,355	44,337	41,126	136,936	1,408
Hardwood	270,758	110,302	15,437	8,271	136,726	22
Total	783,920	399,657	59,774	49,397	273,662	1,430

continued

Table A.8—Industrial roundwood output, by year of survey, species group, and product, North Carolina (continued)

State, year, and species group	All products	Saw logs	Veneer logs	Composite board	Pulpwood	Other industrial[a]
			thousand cubic feet			
North Carolina, 2007						
Softwood	473,704	244,657	35,911	39,403	151,350	2,383
Hardwood	254,680	103,760	14,505	6,356	129,059	1,000
Total	728,384	348,417	50,416	45,759	280,409	3,383
North Carolina, 2009						
Softwood	411,393	183,745	32,871	25,033	167,060	2,684
Hardwood	173,690	70,500	6,130	5,082	90,925	1,053
Total	585,083	254,245	39,001	30,115	257,985	3,737

[a] Includes poles, pilings, posts, and other miscellaneous products.

[b] Pulpwood includes roundwood chipped.

[c] Composite board volume was included with other industrial for 1986 and 1987.

Table A.9—Industrial roundwood output, by year of survey, species group, and product, Oklahoma

State, year, and species group	All products	Saw logs	Veneer logs	Composite board	Pulpwood	Other industrial[a]
	thousand cubic feet					
Oklahoma, 1955						
Softwood	15,550	10,560	0	0	2,540	2,450
Hardwood	6,020	3,160	570	0	340	1,950
Total	21,570	13,720	570	0	2,880	4,400
Oklahoma, 1965						
Softwood	16,620	13,393	0	0	605	2,622
Hardwood	8,986	3,754	70	0	2,371	2,791
Total	25,606	17,147	70	0	2,976	5,413
Oklahoma, 1972						
Softwood	49,642	23,627	6,231	0	15,454	4,330
Hardwood	14,780	4,271	718	0	7,589	2,202
Total	64,422	27,898	6,949	0	23,043	6,532
Oklahoma, 1975						
Softwood	43,072	25,905	5,289	0	8,947	2,931
Hardwood	10,882	5,789	356	0	3,876	861
Total	53,954	31,694	5,645	0	12,823	3,792
Oklahoma, 1978						
Softwood	57,766	24,669	6,030	0	19,713	7,354
Hardwood	15,079	6,444	36	0	8,430	169
Total	72,845	31,113	6,066	0	28,143	7,523
Oklahoma, 1984						
Softwood	41,204	22,254	4,502	0	5,959	8,489
Hardwood	14,123	9,353	87	0	4,145	538
Total	55,327	31,607	4,589	0	10,104	9,027
Oklahoma, 1996[b]						
Softwood	92,989	45,803	12,300	0	28,788	6,098
Hardwood	19,888	8,062	127	0	11,699	0
Total	112,877	53,865	12,427	0	40,487	6,098
Oklahoma, 1999[b]						
Softwood	90,248	42,963	11,469	0	32,508	3,308
Hardwood	29,769	8,543	0	0	21,226	0
Total	120,017	51,506	11,469	0	53,734	3,308
Oklahoma, 2002[b]						
Softwood	97,916	57,304	10,691	0	27,706	2,215
Hardwood	27,865	6,653	0	0	21,212	0
Total	125,781	63,957	10,691	0	48,918	2,215

continued

Table A.9—Industrial roundwood output, by year of survey, species group, and product, Oklahoma (continued)

State, year, and species group	All products	Saw logs	Veneer logs	Composite board	Pulpwood	Other industrial[a]
	thousand cubic feet					
Oklahoma, 2005[b]						
Softwood	95,436	54,691	0	0	19,626	21,119
Hardwood	23,799	6,803	0	0	16,983	13
Total	119,235	61,494	0	0	36,609	21,132
Oklahoma, 2009						
Softwood	46,274	22,759	0	0	19,900	3,615
Hardwood	20,045	2,495	0	0	17,550	0
Total	66,319	25,254	0	0	37,450	3,615

[a] Includes poles, pilings, posts, and other miscellaneous products.

[b] Pulpwood includes roundwood chipped.

Table A.10—Industrial roundwood output, by year of survey, species group, and product, South Carolina

State, year, and species group	All products	Saw logs	Veneer logs	Composite board	Pulpwood	Other industrial[a]
			thousand cubic feet			
South Carolina, 1936						
Softwood	137,650	116,040	2,590	0	2,510	16,510
Hardwood	51,030	29,040	13,400	0	830	7,760
Total	188,680	145,080	15,990	0	3,340	24,270
South Carolina, 1946						
Softwood	229,848	145,872	4,405	0	69,293	10,278
Hardwood	93,018	52,868	25,959	0	7,531	6,660
Total	322,866	198,740	30,364	0	76,824	16,938
South Carolina, 1957						
Softwood	246,900	117,400	600	0	117,100	11,800
Hardwood	87,400	34,400	21,500	0	25,900	5,600
Total	334,300	151,800	22,100	0	143,000	17,400
South Carolina, 1967						
Softwood	253,351	111,572	851	0	131,784	9,144
Hardwood	97,497	42,605	12,135	0	42,325	432
Total	350,848	154,177	12,986	0	174,109	9,576
South Carolina, 1970						
Softwood	268,534	104,222	9,954	0	149,074	5,284
Hardwood	85,014	36,884	9,132	0	38,998	0
Total	353,548	141,106	19,086	0	188,072	5,284
South Carolina, 1971						
Softwood	257,564	104,087	13,434	0	133,634	6,409
Hardwood	84,904	35,364	8,686	0	40,854	0
Total	342,468	139,451	22,120	0	174,488	6,409
South Carolina, 1972						
Softwood	282,203	114,245	14,007	0	147,710	6,241
Hardwood	87,861	39,662	8,644	0	39,555	0
Total	370,064	153,907	22,651	0	187,265	6,241
South Carolina, 1973						
Softwood	296,768	115,634	17,450	0	158,007	5,677
Hardwood	86,900	34,489	9,181	0	43,222	8
Total	383,668	150,123	26,631	0	201,229	5,685
South Carolina, 1974						
Softwood	302,305	105,770	31,938	0	159,825	4,772
Hardwood	87,201	35,389	7,232	0	44,572	8
Total	389,506	141,159	39,170	0	204,397	4,780
South Carolina, 1975						
Softwood	289,554	93,750	34,049	0	158,327	3,428
Hardwood	72,870	29,232	6,452	0	37,178	8
Total	362,424	122,982	40,501	0	195,505	3,436

continued

Table A.10—Industrial roundwood output, by year of survey, species group, and product, South Carolina (continued)

State, year, and species group	All products	Saw logs	Veneer logs	Composite board	Pulpwood	Other industrial[a]
			thousand cubic feet			
South Carolina, 1976						
Softwood	305,693	115,089	37,687	0	149,109	3,808
Hardwood	81,607	32,138	7,397	0	42,048	24
Total	387,300	147,227	45,084	0	191,157	3,832
South Carolina, 1977[b]						
Softwood	355,678	126,865	41,687	0	177,786	9,340
Hardwood	93,903	33,714	6,944	0	53,221	24
Total	449,581	160,579	48,631	0	231,007	9,364
South Carolina, 1978[b]						
Softwood	341,837	130,770	43,847	0	163,314	3,906
Hardwood	106,203	41,716	10,041	0	54,422	24
Total	448,040	172,486	53,888	0	217,736	3,930
South Carolina, 1979[b]						
Softwood	358,038	147,213	40,741	0	166,766	3,318
Hardwood	104,927	40,323	10,416	0	54,188	0
Total	462,965	187,536	51,157	0	220,954	3,318
South Carolina, 1980[b]						
Softwood	347,844	137,496	33,828	0	171,679	4,841
Hardwood	93,545	37,202	8,266	0	48,077	0
Total	441,389	174,698	42,094	0	219,756	4,841
South Carolina, 1981[b]						
Softwood	358,470	129,091	38,541	0	186,830	4,008
Hardwood	88,061	34,642	6,790	0	46,629	0
Total	446,531	163,733	45,331	0	233,459	4,008
South Carolina, 1982[b]						
Softwood	337,673	130,109	35,191	0	168,391	3,982
Hardwood	80,957	27,043	6,087	0	47,827	0
Total	418,630	157,152	41,278	0	216,218	3,982
South Carolina, 1983[b]						
Softwood	375,954	162,377	42,693	0	164,913	5,971
Hardwood	99,673	33,766	8,028	0	57,879	0
Total	475,627	196,143	50,721	0	222,792	5,971
South Carolina, 1984[b]						
Softwood	407,629	182,590	46,280	0	171,222	7,537
Hardwood	121,743	41,997	9,685	0	70,061	0
Total	529,372	224,587	55,965	0	241,283	7,537
South Carolina, 1985[b]						
Softwood	397,311	175,060	45,081	0	169,481	7,689
Hardwood	118,535	41,181	9,620	0	67,734	0
Total	515,846	216,241	54,701	0	237,215	7,689

continued

Table A.10—Industrial roundwood output, by year of survey, species group, and product, South Carolina (continued)

State, year, and species group	All products	Saw logs	Veneer logs	Composite board	Pulpwood	Other industrial[a]
				thousand cubic feet		
South Carolina, 1986[b]						
Softwood	410,532	190,911	49,437	0	165,197	4,987
Hardwood	123,595	35,213	11,047	0	73,716	3,619
Total	534,127	226,124	60,484	0	238,913	8,606
South Carolina, 1987[b]						
Softwood	460,792	205,428	56,413	0	193,216	5,735
Hardwood	129,169	37,228	12,523	0	79,418	0
Total	589,961	242,656	68,936	0	272,634	5,735
South Carolina, 1988[b]						
Softwood	472,454	213,792	51,011	0	202,198	5,453
Hardwood	132,643	39,876	11,665	0	80,975	127
Total	605,097	253,668	62,676	0	283,173	5,580
South Carolina, 1989[b]						
Softwood	458,994	207,730	46,941	0	200,144	4,179
Hardwood	126,702	37,398	10,292	0	78,885	127
Total	585,696	245,128	57,233	0	279,029	4,306
South Carolina, 1990[b]						
Softwood	447,457	198,826	44,740	0	200,214	3,677
Hardwood	119,821	31,851	9,332	0	78,511	127
Total	567,278	230,677	54,072	0	278,725	3,804
South Carolina, 1991[b]						
Softwood	410,616	178,816	44,917	0	183,394	3,489
Hardwood	97,838	24,559	7,017	0	66,262	0
Total	508,454	203,375	51,934	0	249,656	3,489
South Carolina, 1992[b]						
Softwood	472,044	231,538	29,643	0	205,596	5,267
Hardwood	110,418	25,519	6,238	0	78,661	0
Total	582,462	257,057	35,881	0	284,257	5,267
South Carolina, 1994[b]						
Softwood	514,853	229,978	41,957	7	238,111	4,800
Hardwood	138,301	34,510	7,680	37	96,074	0
Total	653,154	264,488	49,637	44	334,185	4,800
South Carolina, 1995[b]						
Softwood	478,475	219,484	42,086	1,302	211,577	4,026
Hardwood	143,507	27,615	7,881	70	107,941	0
Total	621,982	247,099	49,967	1,372	319,518	4,026
South Carolina, 1997[b]						
Softwood	475,819	219,571	40,669	2,593	209,515	3,471
Hardwood	152,362	32,153	7,414	748	112,047	0
Total	628,181	251,724	48,083	3,341	321,562	3,471

continued

Table A.10—Industrial roundwood output, by year of survey, species group, and product, South Carolina (continued)

State, year, and species group	All products	Saw logs	Veneer logs	Composite board	Pulpwood	Other industrial[a]
			thousand cubic feet			
South Carolina, 1999[b]						
Softwood	481,208	209,572	46,938	1,374	219,352	3,972
Hardwood	143,987	32,113	7,536	74	104,264	0
Total	625,195	241,685	54,474	1,448	323,616	3,972
South Carolina, 2001[b]						
Softwood	440,849	191,723	40,967	10,982	193,408	3,769
Hardwood	107,623	24,153	7,025	65	76,380	0
Total	548,472	215,876	47,992	11,047	269,788	3,769
South Carolina, 2003[b]						
Softwood	469,261	207,536	34,781	17,870	205,321	3,753
Hardwood	102,698	27,381	6,958	56	68,303	0
Total	571,959	234,917	41,739	17,926	273,624	3,753
South Carolina, 2005[b]						
Softwood	532,723	233,982	34,299	23,674	236,513	4,255
Hardwood	112,501	23,846	7,324	108	81,223	0
Total	645,224	257,828	41,623	23,782	317,736	4,255
South Carolina, 2007						
Softwood	513,118	204,382	33,091	39,286	230,722	5,637
Hardwood	99,687	22,108	4,705	97	72,777	0
Total	612,805	226,490	37,796	39,383	303,499	5,637
South Carolina, 2009						
Softwood	471,897	134,525	23,948	34,712	265,073	13,639
Hardwood	92,274	14,337	3,777	0	73,000	1,160
Total	564,171	148,862	27,725	34,712	338,073	14,799

[a] Includes poles, pilings, posts, and other miscellaneous products.

[b] Pulpwood includes roundwood chipped.

Table A.11—Industrial roundwood output, by year of survey, species group, and product, Tennessee

State, year, and species group	All products	Saw logs	Veneer logs	Composite board	Pulpwood	Other industrial[a]
			thousand cubic feet			
Tennessee, 1949						
Softwood	48,815	40,410	56	0	4,499	3,850
Hardwood	89,038	58,548	5,787	0	7,654	17,049
Total	137,853	98,958	5,843	0	12,153	20,899
Tennessee, 1960						
Softwood	43,952	27,319	78	0	14,232	2,323
Hardwood	108,749	74,200	5,175	0	12,811	16,563
Total	152,701	101,519	5,253	0	27,043	18,886
Tennessee, 1970						
Softwood	27,904	11,386	30	0	15,398	1,090
Hardwood	109,344	77,486	2,716	0	19,747	9,395
Total	137,248	88,872	2,746	0	35,145	10,485
Tennessee, 1979						
Softwood	33,589	14,215	0	0	18,533	841
Hardwood	144,801	104,286	1,894	0	33,458	5,163
Total	178,390	118,501	1,894	0	51,991	6,004
Tennessee, 1989						
Softwood	65,417	21,786	0	0	43,585	46
Hardwood	177,104	144,721	737	0	30,831	815
Total	242,521	166,507	737	0	74,416	861
Tennessee, 1995						
Softwood	64,585	15,187	9	0	44,838	4,551
Hardwood	219,042	152,369	1,685	0	64,440	548
Total	283,627	167,556	1,694	0	109,278	5,099
Tennessee, 1997						
Softwood	84,595	20,263	122	0	50,813	13,397
Hardwood	236,122	159,278	1,208	0	70,768	4,868
Total	320,717	179,541	1,330	0	121,581	18,265
Tennessee, 1999						
Softwood	100,208	32,928	4,278	0	52,185	10,817
Hardwood	225,035	152,109	1,563	0	68,932	2,431
Total	325,243	185,037	5,841	0	121,117	13,248
Tennessee, 2001						
Softwood	99,117	30,397	271	0	55,183	13,266
Hardwood	225,599	151,914	1,275	0	71,961	449
Total	324,716	182,311	1,546	0	127,144	13,715
Tennessee, 2003						
Softwood	84,812	25,468	294	0	46,031	13,019
Hardwood	227,135	149,992	1,498	0	75,198	447
Total	311,947	175,460	1,792	0	121,229	13,466

continued

Table A.11—Industrial roundwood output, by year of survey, species group, and product, Tennessee (continued)

State, year, and species group	All products	Saw logs	Veneer logs	Composite board	Pulpwood	Other industrial[a]
	thousand cubic feet					
Tennessee, 2005						
Softwood	76,739	27,242	239	0	40,018	9,240
Hardwood	248,550	161,502	1,910	0	81,190	3,948
Total	325,289	188,744	2,149	0	121,208	13,188
Tennessee, 2007						
Softwood	65,026	13,448	0	0	43,360	8,218
Hardwood	232,080	152,316	2,365	0	73,834	3,565
Total	297,106	165,764	2,365	0	117,194	11,783
Tennessee, 2009						
Softwood	47,365	8,029	43	0	37,571	1,722
Hardwood	177,768	97,450	1,218	0	77,945	1,155
Total	225,133	105,479	1,261	0	115,516	2,877

[a] Includes poles, pilings, posts, and other miscellaneous products.

Table A.12—Industrial roundwood output, by year of survey, species group, and product, Texas

State, year, and species group	All products	Saw logs	Veneer logs	Composite board	Pulpwood	Other industrial[a]
			thousand cubic feet			
Texas, 1964						
Softwood	185,624	111,364	1,601	0	63,984	8,675
Hardwood	70,649	41,889	5,709	0	21,889	1,162
Total	256,273	153,253	7,310	0	85,873	9,837
Texas, 1974						
Softwood	374,910	125,847	67,481	0	175,644	5,938
Hardwood	81,551	42,553	3,605	0	34,610	783
Total	456,461	168,400	71,086	0	210,254	6,721
Texas, 1984						
Softwood	406,400	147,500	101,600	0	153,100	4,200
Hardwood	94,200	34,000	1,700	0	58,500	0
Total	500,600	181,500	103,300	0	211,600	4,200
Texas, 1985						
Softwood	386,733	139,331	116,306	0	127,434	3,662
Hardwood	80,728	34,476	1,768	0	44,484	0
Total	467,461	173,807	118,074	0	171,918	3,662
Texas, 1986						
Softwood	437,400	170,100	132,800	0	131,500	3,000
Hardwood	91,500	32,200	2,100	0	57,200	0
Total	528,900	202,300	134,900	0	188,700	3,000
Texas, 1987						
Softwood	447,300	177,300	134,100	0	133,600	2,300
Hardwood	95,400	30,700	2,200	0	62,500	0
Total	542,700	208,000	136,300	0	196,100	2,300
Texas, 1988						
Softwood	459,400	180,900	139,200	0	137,300	2,000
Hardwood	95,700	26,900	3,300	0	65,500	0
Total	555,100	207,800	142,500	0	202,800	2,000
Texas, 1989						
Softwood	462,200	178,100	137,900	0	143,300	2,900
Hardwood	104,800	27,200	2,800	0	74,800	0
Total	567,000	205,300	140,700	0	218,100	2,900
Texas, 1991						
Softwood	460,900	170,000	140,500	0	148,700	1,700
Hardwood	104,500	26,300	2,200	0	76,000	0
Total	565,400	196,300	142,700	0	224,700	1,700
Texas, 1992						
Softwood	496,600	177,500	166,700	0	150,700	1,700
Hardwood	111,300	26,100	2,200	0	83,000	0
Total	607,900	203,600	168,900	0	233,700	1,700

continued

Table A.12—Industrial roundwood output, by year of survey, species group, and product, Texas (continued)

State, year, and species group	All products	Saw logs	Veneer logs	Composite board	Pulpwood	Other industrial[a]
			thousand cubic feet			
Texas, 1993						
Softwood	512,200	182,600	195,700	0	132,500	1,400
Hardwood	121,800	30,500	3,400	0	87,900	0
Total	634,000	213,100	199,100	0	220,400	1,400
Texas, 1994						
Softwood	576,384	232,245	214,754	0	127,487	1,898
Hardwood	139,646	40,497	2,052	0	97,097	0
Total	716,030	272,742	216,806	0	224,584	1,898
Texas, 1995						
Softwood	523,500	192,700	175,000	0	152,200	3,600
Hardwood	143,100	44,900	800	0	97,400	0
Total	666,600	237,600	175,800	0	249,600	3,600
Texas, 1996						
Softwood	543,500	191,200	216,700	0	135,000	600
Hardwood	116,500	50,100	1,100	0	65,300	0
Total	660,000	241,300	217,800	0	200,300	600
Texas, 1997						
Softwood	556,944	180,720	197,333	0	178,537	354
Hardwood	118,483	43,107	998	0	74,378	0
Total	675,427	223,827	198,331	0	252,915	354
Texas, 1998						
Softwood	542,300	194,600	189,800	0	154,700	3,200
Hardwood	136,500	33,100	10,000	0	93,400	0
Total	678,800	227,700	199,800	0	248,100	3,200
Texas, 1999						
Softwood	541,390	201,055	212,737	0	126,677	921
Hardwood	157,831	31,779	2,366	0	123,686	0
Total	699,221	232,834	215,103	0	250,363	921
Texas, 2000						
Softwood	509,000	216,000	196,100	0	96,000	900
Hardwood	135,000	32,300	1,800	0	100,900	0
Total	644,000	248,300	197,900	0	196,900	900
Texas, 2001						
Softwood	488,456	204,172	176,331	0	105,277	2,676
Hardwood	111,413	38,015	1,463	0	71,935	0
Total	599,869	242,187	177,794	0	177,212	2,676
Texas, 2002						
Softwood	537,014	207,403	190,412	0	137,044	2,155
Hardwood	129,643	35,299	413	0	93,931	0
Total	666,657	242,702	190,825	0	230,975	2,155

continued

Table A.12—Industrial roundwood output, by year of survey, species group, and product, Texas (continued)

State, year, and species group	All products	Saw logs	Veneer logs	Composite board	Pulpwood	Other industrial[a]
	thousand cubic feet					
Texas, 2003						
Softwood	542,148	198,832	178,935	0	161,940	2,441
Hardwood	126,119	48,263	20	0	77,836	0
Total	668,267	247,095	178,955	0	239,776	2,441
Texas, 2004						
Softwood	517,671	210,402	182,447	0	122,727	2,095
Hardwood	133,460	47,512	0	0	85,948	0
Total	651,131	257,914	182,447	0	208,675	2,095
Texas, 2005						
Softwood	564,268	237,699	194,772	0	129,468	2,329
Hardwood	137,175	41,987	493	0	94,695	0
Total	701,443	279,686	195,265	0	224,163	2,329
Texas, 2006						
Softwood	500,049	201,010	180,980	0	114,694	3,365
Hardwood	148,306	41,466	456	0	106,384	0
Total	648,355	242,476	181,436	0	221,078	3,365
Texas, 2007						
Softwood	501,201	199,402	163,637	0	135,401	2,761
Hardwood	127,620	32,166	570	0	94,867	17
Total	628,821	231,568	164,207	0	230,268	2,778
Texas, 2008						
Softwood	440,281	185,942	103,153	0	148,488	2,698
Hardwood	97,684	37,252	528	0	59,904	0
Total	537,965	223,194	103,681	0	208,392	2,698
Texas, 2009						
Softwood	396,404	165,930	91,028	0	137,590	1,856
Hardwood	83,437	34,168	528	0	48,741	0
Total	479,841	200,098	91,556	0	186,331	1,856

[a] Includes poles, pilings, posts, and other miscellaneous products.

Table A.13—Industrial roundwood output, by year of survey, species group, and product, Virginia

State, year, and species group	All products	Saw logs	Veneer logs	Composite board	Pulpwood	Other industrial[a]
			thousand cubic feet			
Virginia, 1940						
Softwood	155,106	105,479	4,413	0	45,090	124
Hardwood	63,949	52,383	4,852	0	6,653	61
Total	219,055	157,862	9,265	0	51,743	185
Virginia, 1956						
Softwood	225,837	110,896	11,958	0	85,305	17,678
Hardwood	153,438	116,454	1,920	0	25,312	9,752
Total	379,275	227,350	13,878	0	110,617	27,430
Virginia, 1965						
Softwood	184,554	82,300	217	0	93,840	8,197
Hardwood	165,336	99,424	7,214	0	49,980	8,718
Total	349,890	181,724	7,431	0	143,820	16,915
Virginia, 1967[b]						
Softwood	171,882	75,202	3,847	0	84,192	8,641
Hardwood	159,773	93,752	6,965	0	49,970	9,086
Total	331,655	168,954	10,812	0	134,162	17,727
Virginia, 1976[b]						
Softwood	166,223	80,157	8,273	0	73,875	3,918
Hardwood	189,835	109,129	2,693	0	75,064	2,949
Total	356,058	189,286	10,966	0	148,939	6,867
Virginia, 1978[b]						
Softwood	172,646	91,443	9,390	0	67,936	3,877
Hardwood	187,225	108,349	4,273	0	70,884	3,719
Total	359,871	199,792	13,663	0	138,820	7,596
Virginia, 1980[b]						
Softwood	185,324	91,929	6,369	0	84,996	2,030
Hardwood	194,760	109,238	3,022	0	79,746	2,754
Total	380,084	201,167	9,391	0	164,742	4,784
Virginia, 1984[b c]						
Softwood	215,614	92,533	15,056	0	102,555	5,470
Hardwood	247,642	131,921	4,182	0	109,171	2,368
Total	463,256	224,454	19,238	0	211,726	7,838
Virginia, 1987[b c]						
Softwood	200,384	106,536	11,709	0	74,810	7,329
Hardwood	212,132	125,643	5,122	0	75,762	5,605
Total	412,516	232,179	16,831	0	150,572	12,934
Virginia, 1989[b]						
Softwood	205,502	92,035	11,196	4,572	94,278	3,421
Hardwood	230,175	130,559	4,448	8,611	83,555	3,002
Total	435,677	222,594	15,644	13,183	177,833	6,423

continued

Table A.13—Industrial roundwood output, by year of survey, species group, and product, Virginia (continued)

State, year, and species group	All products	Saw logs	Veneer logs	Composite board	Pulpwood	Other industrial[a]
				thousand cubic feet		
Virginia, 1992[b]						
Softwood	220,442	92,552	12,851	6,546	105,052	3,441
Hardwood	215,952	113,003	5,054	9,288	84,359	4,248
Total	436,394	205,555	17,905	15,834	189,411	7,689
Virginia, 1995[b]						
Softwood	231,962	93,769	13,134	10,089	113,741	1,229
Hardwood	223,658	119,000	3,163	11,373	87,624	2,498
Total	455,620	212,769	16,297	21,462	201,365	3,727
Virginia, 1999[b]						
Softwood	260,427	115,299	13,947	31,106	97,664	2,411
Hardwood	231,134	130,578	5,947	14,552	77,536	2,521
Total	491,561	245,877	19,894	45,658	175,200	4,932
Virginia, 2001[b]						
Softwood	253,922	115,703	13,075	34,066	89,200	1,878
Hardwood	237,993	136,729	5,810	13,779	81,246	429
Total	491,915	252,432	18,885	47,845	170,446	2,307
Virginia, 2003[b]						
Softwood	251,711	108,085	8,401	44,584	89,198	1,443
Hardwood	236,446	121,180	8,448	9,125	97,264	429
Total	488,157	229,265	16,849	53,709	186,462	1,872
Virginia, 2005[b]						
Softwood	268,473	106,728	11,265	53,151	96,316	1,013
Hardwood	234,307	121,439	4,915	4,176	103,385	392
Total	502,780	228,167	16,180	57,327	199,701	1,405
Virginia, 2007						
Softwood	253,394	99,859	12,754	50,556	84,676	5,549
Hardwood	210,613	119,406	4,142	3,564	77,604	5,897
Total	464,007	219,265	16,896	54,120	162,280	11,446
Virginia, 2009						
Softwood	224,686	83,130	6,974	42,525	86,171	5,886
Hardwood	177,777	91,728	2,867	1,481	72,039	9,662
Total	402,463	174,858	9,841	44,006	158,210	15,548

[a] Includes poles, pilings, posts, and other miscellaneous products.

[b] Pulpwood includes roundwood chipped.

[c] Composite board volume was included with other industrial for 1984 and 1987.

Table A.14—Number of primary wood-using plants by type of mill, Alabama, 1951 to 2009

Type of mill	Year											
	1951	1962	1971	1982	1985	1995	1997	1999	2003	2005	2007	2009
	number											
Sawmills	1,450	555	323	239	250	148	145	121	118	93	93	78
Veneer mills	42	34	32	28	28	23	26	23	23	19	18	12
Pulpmills	7	9	15	16	16	16	16	15	14	14	14	13
Composite panel mills	0	0	0	0	0	1	1	1	2	2	2	1
Other mills	71	47	36	35	47	23	24	21	21	17	17	16
All plants	1,570	645	406	318	341	211	212	181	178	145	144	120

Table A.15—Number of primary wood-using plants by type of mill, Arkansas, 1948 to 2009

Type of mill	Year											
	1948	1958	1968	1971	1977	1987	1996	1999	2002	2005	2007	2009
	number											
Sawmills	1,736	974	448	278	384	274	286	308	260	139	127	75
Veneer or plywood mills	23	11	12	13	8	8	10	10	10	9	7	5
Pulpmills	2	4	7	7	8	8	8	8	6	6	6	6
Composite panel mills	0	0	0	0	0	0	0	0	1	1	1	1
Other mills	146	79	104	108	72	35	15	10	11	1	0	3
All plants	1,907	1,068	571	406	472	325	319	336	288	156	141	90

Table A.16—Number of primary wood-using plants by type of mill, Florida, 1958 to 2009

Type of mill	Year																			
	1958	1969	1971	1973	1975	1977	1979	1983	1986	1987	1989	1991	1993	1995	1997	1999	2003	2005	2007	2009
	number																			
Sawmills	105	91	88	85	92	104	112	108	106	97	85	71	64	68	58	53	53	53	37	28
Veneer mills	17	17	14	14	9	10	10	10	6	5	5	5	5	5	5	4	3	3	3	3
Pulpmills	10	9	9	10	10	10	10	9	9	10	9	9	8	8	8	6	6	6	6	6
Composite panel mills	0	0	0	0	0	0	0	0	0	0	0	0	0	0	0	0	0	1	1	1
Other mills	28	22	21	14	14	16	16	16	30	31	28	30	32	32	30	30	30	30	22	21
All plants	160	139	132	123	125	140	148	143	151	143	127	115	109	113	101	93	92	93	69	59

Table A.17—Number of primary wood-using plants by type of mill, Georgia, 1952 to 2009

Type of mill	Year																	
	1952	1961	1971	1974	1977	1980	1983	1986	1989	1992	1995	1997	1999	2001	2003	2005	2007	2009
	number																	
Sawmills	725	527	301	301	280	265	222	239	172	178	144	129	129	118	122	115	105	88
Veneer mills	27	27	23	24	23	22	19	18	16	14	12	11	12	10	8	8	7	6
Pulpmills	7	12	15	15	15	15	15	15	14	13	14	13	12	13	12	12	12	12
Composite panel mills	0	0	0	0	0	0	0	0	3	4	5	5	4	4	4	4	4	3
Other mills	38	32	29	26	26	25	28	29	26	41	32	28	31	25	41	42	40	43
All plants	797	598	368	366	344	327	284	301	231	250	207	186	188	170	187	181	168	152

Table A.18—Number of primary wood-using plants by type of mill, Kentucky, 1948 to 2009

Type of mill	Year												
	1948	1964	1969	1974	1986	1995	1997	1999	2003	2005	2005	2007	2009
	number												
Sawmills	2,168	620	538	388	408	376	365	330	317	282	277	241	217
Veneer mills	6	3	4	4	3	3	4	3	3	3	3	3	1
Pulpmills	0	0	2	2	2	2	2	2	2	2	2	2	2
Composite panel mills	0	0	0	0	0	1	1	1	1	1	1	1	0
Other mills	90	30	45	26	22	19	19	12	14	9	9	6	5
All plants	2,264	653	589	420	435	401	391	348	337	297	292	253	225

Table A.19—Number of primary wood-using plants by type of mill, Louisiana, 1937 to 2009

Type of mill	Year									
	1937	1953	1962	1963	1996	1999	2002	2005	2007	2009
	number									
Sawmills	557	458	160	164	70	32	35	37	35	23
Veneer or plywood mills	15	15	11	11	14	10	10	11	9	7
Pulpmills	6	8	10	10	11	11	11	10	10	8
Composite panel and other mills	65	49	36	38	5	4	4	4	2	3
All plants	643	530	217	223	100	57	60	62	56	41

Table A.20—Number of primary wood-using plants by type of mill, Mississippi, 1946 to 2009

Type of mill	Year											
	1946	1956	1962	1966	1972	1976	1995	1999	2002	2005	2007	2009
	number											
Sawmills	2,000	1,000	290	305	241	218	84	84	92	93	66	57
Veneer mills	30	28	24	22	16	13	10	10	12	12	8	7
Pulpmills	6	6	6	7	8	7	7	7	6	5	5	5
Composite panel mills	0	0	0	0	0	0	2	2	3	3	2	2
Other mills	60	54	64	74	50	55	2	2	3	3	3	2
All plants	2,096	1,088	384	408	315	293	105	105	116	116	84	73

Table A.21—Number of primary wood-using plants by type of mill, North Carolina, 1955 to 2009

Type of mill	Year																		
	1955	1964	1973	1976	1979	1983	1986	1987	1990	1992	1994	1995	1997	1999	2001	2003	2005	2007	2009
	number																		
Sawmills	755	555	355	403	478	429	336	362	308	306	275	273	243	240	215	204	153	136	118
Veneer mills	62	60	36	32	31	33	32	31	32	29	27	27	23	24	20	18	14	14	10
Pulpmills	5	5	8	8	8	8	8	8	8	8	8	8	7	7	7	6	6	6	6
Composite panel mills	0	0	0	0	0	0	4	4	5	4	4	4	3	3	3	3	3	2	2
Other mills	39	30	11	9	13	14	15	17	13	10	8	8	4	4	4	4	4	5	5
All plants	861	650	410	452	530	484	395	422	366	357	322	320	280	278	249	235	180	163	141

Table A.22—Number of primary wood-using plants by type of mill, Oklahoma, 1955 to 2009

Type of mill	Year										
	1955	1965	1972	1975	1978	1984	1996	1999	2002	2005	2009
	number										
Sawmills	80	110	103	83	66	84	68	62	97	95	26
Veneer or plywood mills	1	0	1	1	1	1	1	1	1	1	0
Pulpmills	1	2	3	3	3	3	2	2	2	2	1
Composite panel mills	0	0	0	0	0	0	0	0	1	1	2
Other mills	17	19	11	14	11	12	2	2	8	8	2
All plants	99	131	118	101	81	100	73	67	109	107	31

Table A.23—Number of primary wood-using plants by type of mill, South Carolina, 1957 to 2009

Type of mill	Year																								
	1957	1967	1970	1972	1973	1974	1975	1976	1977	1979	1983	1985	1987	1989	1992	1994	1995	1997	1999	2001	2003	2005	2007	2009
	number																							
Sawmills	265	239	206	150	152	152	133	132	119	128	113	118	99	87	79	76	70	66	63	51	51	48	44	39
Veneer mills	27	26	27	24	24	22	26	26	23	24	21	21	20	17	14	14	14	12	12	9	8	8	8	6
Pulpmills	3	5	6	6	6	6	7	7	7	7	8	8	8	8	9	8	8	8	7	7	7	7	7	7
Composite panel mills	0	0	0	0	0	0	0	0	0	0	0	0	0	0	0	0	0	0	0	1	1	1	2	2
Other mills	14	13	9	7	7	8	8	8	5	4	6	8	6	5	9	7	7	6	8	8	8	11	14	23
All plants	309	283	248	187	189	188	174	173	154	163	148	155	133	117	111	105	99	92	90	76	75	75	75	77

Table A.24—Number of primary wood-using plants by type of mill, Tennessee, 1949 to 2009

Type of mill	Year											
	1949	1960	1970	1979	1989	1995	1997	1999	2001	2005	2007	2009
	number											
Sawmills	2,789	1,135	546	694	490	495	496	440	439	345	320	257
Veneer mills	14	9	6	5	3	2	2	2	2	1	1	1
Pulpmills	4	5	7	7	6	5	5	5	5	5	5	5
Composite panel mills	0	0	0	0	0	0	1	1	1	1	1	1
Other mills	177	133	64	32	24	1	1	3	3	2	2	3
All plants	2,984	1,282	623	738	523	503	505	451	450	354	329	267

Table A.25—Number of primary wood-using plants by type of mill, Texas, 1957 to 2009

Type of mill	Year															
	1954	1964	1974	1986	1987	1989	1991	1993	1995	1997	1999	2001	2003	2005	2007	2009[a]
	number															
Sawmills	496	177	139	71	75	68	62	64	61	55	49	58	53	53	78	81
Veneer mills	10	16	20	14	4	4	4	4	4	3	3	2	2	2	5	5
Pulpmills	2	5	8	8	7	7	7	7	7	7	6	5	5	4	4	4
Composite panel mills	0	0	0	1	11	11	12	12	12	12	10	9	8	9	5	4
Other mills	50	41	35	23	23	29	27	27	27	23	19	14	14	15	15	8
All plants	558	239	202	117	120	119	112	114	111	100	87	88	82	83	107	102

[a] Counted more mills in west Texas.

Table A.26—Number of primary wood-using plants by type of mill, Virginia, 1956 to 2009

Type of mill	Year															
	1956	1965	1976	1978	1980	1984	1987	1989	1992	1995	1999	2001	2003	2005	2007	2009
	number															
Sawmills	1,200	870	451	324	392	419	355	323	276	254	254	217	204	168	155	129
Veneer or plywood mills	25	23	10	12	12	12	10	10	9	8	7	5	5	4	4	3
Pulpmills	8	7	9	8	9	9	9	9	9	9	9	9	9	8	8	8
Composite panel mills	0	0	0	0	0	0	1	3	3	3	4	3	3	3	3	3
Other mills	47	45	15	18	24	22	19	24	14	15	16	14	13	13	9	8
All plants	1,280	945	485	362	437	462	394	369	311	289	290	248	234	196	179	151

Table A.27—Forest sector direct and total effect in employment by State, 2004–09

State	Effect	Year					Change	Change
		2004	2006	2007	2008	2009		
		- - - - - - - - - - - - - - - *number of jobs (full- and part-time)* - - - - - - - - - - - - - - -						*percent*
Alabama	Direct	53,675	55,826	53,836	53,480	39,279	-14,396	-27
	Total	112,551	113,773	114,056	106,589	88,667	-23,885	-21
Arkansas	Direct	35,341	34,520	32,446	33,145	27,041	-8,300	-23
	Total	78,105	75,166	65,793	65,119	54,488	-23,617	-30
Florida	Direct	47,520	51,103	43,955	43,521	32,788	-14,733	-31
	Total	112,282	122,729	111,086	112,133	86,343	-25,939	-23
Georgia	Direct	65,208	66,980	63,679	64,514	49,114	-16,094	-25
	Total	149,521	151,472	151,273	146,322	123,429	-26,092	-17
Kentucky	Direct	30,463	30,932	30,681	29,893	23,848	-6,615	-22
	Total	58,684	58,350	57,702	55,264	46,137	-12,546	-21
Louisiana	Direct	24,721	25,169	24,691	24,819	19,213	-5,508	-22
	Total	59,494	57,098	55,357	53,813	43,592	-15,901	-27
Mississippi	Direct	28,747	30,299	29,543	29,925	21,704	-7,043	-24
	Total	57,953	59,249	54,949	54,762	40,580	-17,374	-30
North Carolina	Direct	77,177	74,167	70,135	67,559	50,108	-27,069	-35
	Total	144,657	142,181	146,590	137,041	108,010	-36,647	-25
Oklahoma	Direct	10,204	10,330	9,863	9,994	7,530	-2,674	-26
	Total	24,794	24,663	20,879	20,478	16,759	-8,035	-32
South Carolina	Direct	31,432	32,654	31,767	32,897	26,660	-4,772	-15
	Total	66,995	69,487	72,903	72,553	64,134	-2,861	-4
Tennessee	Direct	44,655	45,979	43,222	43,873	34,058	-10,597	-24
	Total	98,670	101,237	98,700	97,035	83,928	-14,742	-15
Texas	Direct	73,753	78,713	74,724	77,310	59,501	-14,252	-19
	Total	152,339	158,545	165,387	166,553	138,483	-13,856	-9
Virginia	Direct	50,341	50,603	46,932	47,465	34,282	-16,059	-32
	Total	90,743	91,783	91,304	88,125	68,465	-22,279	-25
Total	Direct	573,237	587,274	555,475	558,394	425,125	-148,111	-26
	Total	1,206,788	1,225,734	1,205,980	1,175,786	963,015	-243,773	-20

Source: IMpact analysis for PLANning (IMPLAN) V3.0.

Table A.28—Forest sector direct and total effect in labor income by State, 2004–09

State	Effect	Year					Change	Change
		2004	2006	2007	2008	2009		
		- - - - - - - - - - - - - - - - - millions of dollars - - - - - - - - - - - - - - - - -						percent
Alabama	Direct	$3,176	$3,392	$3,203	$3,218	$2,409	$-767	-24
	Total	5,462	5,696	5,656	5,394	4,395	-1,067	-20
Arkansas	Direct	1,849	1,830	1,659	1,695	1,489	-361	-20
	Total	3,416	3,332	2,964	3,005	2,652	-764	-22
Florida	Direct	2,530	2,846	2,342	2,355	1,736	-794	-31
	Total	5,042	5,651	5,260	5,171	4,049	-993	-20
Georgia	Direct	3,923	4,083	3,698	3,751	3,039	-883	-23
	Total	7,805	7,913	7,934	7,648	6,558	-1,247	-16
Kentucky	Direct	1,499	1,561	1,492	1,495	1,220	-279	-19
	Total	2,627	2,684	2,596	2,562	2,152	-475	-18
Louisiana	Direct	1,581	1,605	1,546	1,570	1,309	-272	-17
	Total	2,903	2,821	2,832	2,841	2,343	-560	-19
Mississippi	Direct	1,499	1,568	1,491	1,539	1,154	-345	-23
	Total	2,514	2,589	2,404	2,437	1,860	-654	-26
North Carolina	Direct	3,888	3,967	3,576	3,535	2,739	-1,149	-30
	Total	6,674	6,791	6,842	6,522	5,229	-1,445	-22
Oklahoma	Direct	533	528	485	510	416	-117	-22
	Total	1,060	1,055	941	965	809	-251	-24
South Carolina	Direct	1,936	2,188	2,041	2,073	1,753	-182	-9
	Total	3,314	3,620	3,695	3,686	3,239	-75	-2
Tennessee	Direct	2,795	2,973	2,639	2,950	2,226	-569	-20
	Total	5,223	5,494	5,221	5,458	4,522	-701	-13
Texas	Direct	4,200	4,631	4,391	4,639	3,371	-829	-20
	Total	7,830	8,450	8,960	9,081	7,166	-664	-8
Virginia	Direct	2,572	2,703	2,396	2,484	1,910	-662	-26
	Total	4,431	4,642	4,645	4,542	3,652	-779	-18
Total	Direct	31,981	33,874	30,960	31,814	24,771	-7,209	-23
	Total	58,301	60,737	59,951	59,313	48,625	-9,676	-17

Source: IMpact analysis for PLANning (IMPLAN) V3.0.

Table A. 29—Forest sector direct and total effect in production output by State, 2004–09

State	Effect	Year					Change	Change
		2004	2006	2007	2008	2009		
		- - - - - - - - - - - - - - - - - - *millions of dollars* - - - - - - - - - - - - - - - - - -						*percent*
Alabama	Direct	$16,840	$17,490	$17,098	$16,379	$12,726	$-4,115	-24
	Total	24,228	25,133	24,915	23,457	18,956	-5,273	-22
Arkansas	Direct	11,636	11,404	10,793	10,714	8,917	-2,719	-23
	Total	16,609	16,406	14,812	14,665	12,351	-4,258	-26
Florida	Direct	12,695	13,762	11,961	11,675	9,026	-3,669	-29
	Total	19,785	21,700	20,478	19,860	15,534	-4,252	-21
Georgia	Direct	21,573	22,087	21,062	20,786	16,592	-4,981	-23
	Total	33,275	33,819	33,624	32,490	26,830	-6,445	-19
Kentucky	Direct	8,098	8,190	8,154	8,048	6,556	-1,543	-19
	Total	11,734	11,941	11,605	11,395	9,399	-2,335	-20
Louisiana	Direct	9,065	9,124	9,019	8,599	6,627	-2,438	-27
	Total	13,524	13,418	13,243	12,796	9,949	-3,574	-26
Mississippi	Direct	8,531	8,938	8,486	8,081	5,607	-2,924	-34
	Total	11,753	12,359	11,298	10,887	7,772	-3,982	-34
North Carolina	Direct	19,385	19,586	18,570	17,763	13,647	-5,738	-30
	Total	28,017	28,669	28,459	26,804	20,872	-7,145	-26
Oklahoma	Direct	3,091	3,072	3,034	3,065	2,442	-649	-21
	Total	4,737	4,739	4,515	4,531	3,692	-1,045	-22
South Carolina	Direct	10,837	11,634	11,474	11,797	9,940	-897	-8
	Total	15,234	16,269	16,543	16,769	14,414	-820	-5
Tennessee	Direct	14,238	14,908	14,205	14,432	11,710	-2,528	-18
	Total	21,803	22,991	21,949	22,188	18,546	-3,257	-15
Texas	Direct	19,920	20,962	20,497	20,344	15,812	-4,107	-21
	Total	31,371	33,517	34,887	34,738	27,873	-3,498	-11
Virginia	Direct	12,987	13,311	12,661	12,400	9,294	-3,693	-28
	Total	18,633	19,328	19,335	18,691	14,369	-4,264	-23
Total	Direct	168,896	174,470	167,013	164,084	128,896	-40,000	-24
	Total	250,703	260,291	255,663	249,270	200,556	-50,147	-20

Source: IMpact analysis for PLANning (IMPLAN) V3.0.

Table A.30—Forest sector direct effect in employment by State and major forest sector group, 2004–09

State	Forest sector group	Year 2004	2006	2007	2008	2009	Change	Change
		------------- *number of jobs (full- and part-time)* -------------						*percent*
Alabama	Inputs	7,997	8,110	8,697	8,751	6,803	-1,195	-15
	Solid, primary	7,791	8,024	6,614	6,577	4,939	-2,851	-37
	Panel	3,383	3,570	3,323	3,284	1,749	-1,634	-48
	Pulp and paper	10,430	9,910	9,672	9,774	8,985	-1,445	-14
	Solid, secondary	20,031	22,082	21,516	20,993	13,341	-6,689	-33
	Pulp and paper products	4,044	4,130	4,014	4,102	3,462	-582	-14
Arkansas	Inputs	5,787	5,699	6,161	6,660	5,161	-626	-11
	Solid, primary	7,474	7,656	5,586	5,578	4,582	-2,892	-39
	Panel	2,880	3,082	2,728	2,707	2,229	-651	-23
	Pulp and paper	4,638	4,490	4,163	4,327	4,125	-513	-11
	Solid, secondary	7,247	6,556	7,087	7,298	4,717	-2,530	-35
	Pulp and paper products	7,315	7,037	6,722	6,576	6,227	-1,088	-15
Florida	Inputs	4,205	4,698	4,786	4,879	6,121	1,915	46
	Solid, primary	3,223	3,181	2,701	2,750	2,088	-1,135	-35
	Panel	1,197	1,180	1,126	1,205	1,071	-126	-11
	Pulp and paper	2,920	2,799	2,780	2,830	2,691	-228	-8
	Solid, secondary	28,534	31,634	25,447	24,429	14,225	-14,309	-50
	Pulp and paper products	7,441	7,611	7,115	7,427	6,591	-851	-11
Georgia	Inputs	8,458	9,106	9,460	9,787	7,563	-895	-11
	Solid, primary	6,431	7,154	6,701	7,383	5,828	-602	-9
	Panel	3,849	3,864	3,486	3,262	2,393	-1,457	-38
	Pulp and paper	9,582	8,702	8,238	8,501	7,892	-1,690	-18
	Solid, secondary	22,264	24,110	23,161	23,069	14,375	-7,890	-35
	Pulp and paper products	14,624	14,045	12,631	12,512	11,063	-3,560	-24
Kentucky	Inputs	2,449	2,397	2,739	2,512	2,050	-399	-16
	Solid, primary	5,050	5,221	3,475	3,438	2,548	-2,502	-50
	Panel	672	804	798	772	471	-201	-30
	Pulp and paper	1,717	1,629	1,603	1,600	1,549	-168	-10
	Solid, secondary	12,386	13,033	13,570	13,209	9,633	-2,753	-22
	Pulp and paper products	8,189	7,847	8,497	8,361	7,596	-593	-7
Louisiana	Inputs	5,038	5,036	5,394	5,947	4,450	-589	-12
	Solid, primary	2,620	2,902	2,792	2,819	2,061	-559	-21
	Panel	4,384	4,634	4,363	4,168	2,043	-2,341	-53
	Pulp and paper	5,906	5,248	4,847	4,631	3,841	-2,066	-35
	Solid, secondary	3,131	3,737	3,785	3,802	3,600	470	15
	Pulp and paper products	3,642	3,613	3,510	3,452	3,219	-423	-12
Mississippi	Inputs	6,725	6,953	7,281	7,396	5,554	-1,171	-17
	Solid, primary	6,784	6,976	5,610	5,594	4,222	-2,562	-38
	Panel	3,360	3,676	3,618	3,620	2,430	-930	-28
	Pulp and paper	2,258	2,114	2,015	2,080	1,907	-352	-16
	Solid, secondary	6,295	7,650	8,197	8,530	5,246	-1,049	-17
	Pulp and paper products	3,325	2,930	2,822	2,704	2,345	-980	-29

continued

Table A.30—Forest sector direct effect in employment by State and major forest sector group, 2004–09 (continued)

State	Forest sector group	Year 2004	2006	2007	2008	2009	Change	Change
		- - - - - - - - - - - - - number of jobs (full- and part-time) - - - - - - - - - - - - - -						*percent*
North Carolina	Inputs	6,235	6,188	6,963	6,709	5,453	-781	-13
	Solid, primary	6,931	6,880	5,719	5,497	4,270	-2,661	-38
	Panel	6,334	6,021	5,473	4,849	3,284	-3,051	-48
	Pulp and paper	5,671	5,360	5,103	5,011	4,444	-1,227	-22
	Solid, secondary	38,803	36,407	33,646	31,909	20,683	-18,119	-47
	Pulp and paper products	13,203	13,310	13,230	13,584	11,973	-1,229	-9
Oklahoma	Inputs	953	1,135	1,279	1,154	938	-15	-2
	Solid, primary	1,687	1,373	1,253	1,235	918	-769	-46
	Panel	191	236	209	130	123	-68	-36
	Pulp and paper	916	943	1,916	2,021	1,852	936	102
	Solid, secondary	4,121	4,719	4,268	4,496	2,885	-1,235	-30
	Pulp and paper products	2,336	1,925	938	958	815	-1,521	-65
South Carolina	Inputs	5,134	5,027	5,289	5,401	4,290	-845	-16
	Solid, primary	3,633	4,148	3,813	3,754	2,867	-767	-21
	Panel	2,265	2,230	2,256	2,349	1,900	-364	-16
	Pulp and paper	4,925	4,767	4,702	4,796	4,312	-613	-12
	Solid, secondary	6,500	7,497	7,142	7,873	4,879	-1,621	-25
	Pulp and paper products	8,974	8,984	8,567	8,724	8,412	-561	-6
Tennessee	Inputs	2,993	3,013	3,913	3,516	3,073	80	3
	Solid, primary	5,528	5,753	4,400	4,055	3,070	-2,459	-44
	Panel	612	661	395	345	155	-457	-75
	Pulp and paper	6,430	6,478	6,149	6,340	5,820	-609	-9
	Solid, secondary	17,013	18,406	17,639	18,749	12,016	-4,996	-29
	Pulp and paper products	12,079	11,668	10,726	10,868	9,923	-2,156	-18
Texas	Inputs	4,599	4,809	5,440	5,625	4,570	-29	-1
	Solid, primary	4,999	5,172	4,413	4,780	3,831	-1,167	-23
	Panel	4,121	4,452	4,011	3,683	3,210	-911	-22
	Pulp and paper	3,833	3,282	3,336	3,362	2,990	-843	-22
	Solid, secondary	38,181	43,922	41,235	43,853	30,256	-7,926	-21
	Pulp and paper products	18,020	17,074	16,289	16,007	14,645	-3,375	-19
Virginia	Inputs	3,971	4,221	4,754	4,731	3,669	-303	-8
	Solid, primary	6,234	6,411	5,095	5,311	4,051	-2,183	-35
	Panel	2,567	3,023	2,717	2,745	1,919	-648	-25
	Pulp and paper	5,068	4,931	4,793	4,852	4,302	-766	-15
	Solid, secondary	26,280	26,122	23,686	23,978	15,534	-10,746	-41
	Pulp and paper products	6,220	5,894	5,888	5,849	4,806	-1,414	-23
Total	Inputs	64,545.0	66,393.3	72,156.5	73,066.9	59,691.8	-4,853	-8
	Solid, primary	68,384.3	70,851.4	58,171.1	58,770.5	45,276.1	-23,108	-34
	Panel	35,816.6	37,433.5	34,502.80	33,119.5	22,977.8	-12,839	-36
	Pulp and paper	64,294.8	60,652.6	59,317.4	60,124.6	54,710.5	-9,584	-15
	Solid, secondary	230,785.5	245,874.0	230,378.6	232,188.0	151,392.0	-79,394	-34
	Pulp and paper products	109,410.5	106,069.5	100,948.1	101,124.3	91,077.2	-18,333	-17

Source: IMpact analysis for PLANning (IMPLAN) V3.0.

63

Table A.31—Forest sector direct effect in labor income by State and major forest sector group, 2004–09

State	Forest sector group	Year					Change	Change
		2004	2006	2007	2008	2009		
		- - - - - - - - - - - - - - - *millions of dollars* - - - - - - - - - - - - - - -						*percent*
Alabama	Inputs	$419	$384	$391	$402	$330	$-89	-21
	Solid, primary	363	367	311	309	230	-133	-37
	Panel	180	181	170	167	91	-90	-50
	Pulp and paper	1,194	1,261	1,237	1,261	1,015	-179	-15
	Solid, secondary	754	901	805	775	504	-250	-33
	Pulp and paper products	266	298	290	304	240	-26	-10
Arkansas	Inputs	262	216	236	254	201	-61	-23
	Solid, primary	321	330	245	252	205	-116	-36
	Panel	145	148	141	141	131	-14	-10
	Pulp and paper	440	460	394	405	397	-43	-10
	Solid, secondary	251	238	243	252	175	-76	-30
	Pulp and paper products	430	437	401	392	380	-50	-12
Florida	Inputs	194	203	188	192	176	-18	-9
	Solid, primary	152	148	123	115	88	-64	-42
	Panel	61	58	56	62	57	-4	-7
	Pulp and paper	330	328	325	339	293	-37	-11
	Solid, secondary	1,230	1,487	1,091	1,057	632	-598	-49
	Pulp and paper products	563	622	560	590	491	-72	-13
Georgia	Inputs	417	431	435	432	373	-45	-11
	Solid, primary	296	326	299	334	278	-17	-6
	Panel	232	225	187	174	138	-95	-41
	Pulp and paper	1,027	1,021	899	954	831	-197	-19
	Solid, secondary	907	1,026	936	925	604	-303	-33
	Pulp and paper products	1,043	1,054	943	932	816	-227	-22
Kentucky	Inputs	67	50	57	65	47	-20	-29
	Solid, primary	164	168	109	112	79	-85	-52
	Panel	22	27	28	28	16	-6	-27
	Pulp and paper	172	164	155	163	154	-18	-10
	Solid, secondary	518	603	573	556	426	-92	-18
	Pulp and paper products	557	550	570	570	498	-59	-11
Louisiana	Inputs	251	226	260	284	235	-16	-7
	Solid, primary	130	142	137	143	113	-17	-13
	Panel	238	242	232	228	121	-117	-49
	Pulp and paper	604	591	538	528	466	-138	-23
	Solid, secondary	109	148	144	146	159	50	46
	Pulp and paper products	249	256	234	241	215	-34	-14
Mississippi	Inputs	309	292	300	319	257	-52	-17
	Solid, primary	307	317	253	252	194	-114	-37
	Panel	189	191	190	187	131	-58	-30
	Pulp and paper	261	271	254	265	224	-37	-14
	Solid, secondary	212	295	297	317	204	-8	-4
	Pulp and paper products	221	203	196	197	144	-77	-35

continued

Table A.31—Forest sector direct effect in labor income by State and major forest sector group, 2004–09 (continued)

State	Forest sector group	Year 2004	2006	2007	2008	2009	Change	Change percent
		- - - - - - - - - - - - - - *millions of dollars* - - - - - - - - - - - - - - -						*percent*
North Carolina	Inputs	276	240	257	266	223	-53	-19
	Solid, primary	294	286	246	236	183	-110	-38
	Panel	292	279	257	234	169	-124	-42
	Pulp and paper	533	556	516	518	440	-93	-17
	Solid, secondary	1,601	1,650	1,389	1,319	918	-683	-43
	Pulp and paper products	892	955	913	962	806	-86	-10
Oklahoma	Inputs	45	31	41	44	32	-13	-28
	Solid, primary	100	81	76	83	65	-35	-35
	Panel	7	7	7	5	5	-2	-27
	Pulp and paper	70	79	155	162	157	87	126
	Solid, secondary	151	172	150	158	107	-44	-29
	Pulp and paper products	160	158	56	58	49	-111	-69
South Carolina	Inputs	224	205	209	213	189	-35	-16
	Solid, primary	166	211	172	179	139	-27	-16
	Panel	110	112	119	128	113	3	3
	Pulp and paper	509	579	530	528	443	-66	-13
	Solid, secondary	232	310	291	308	199	-33	-14
	Pulp and paper products	695	770	719	717	670	-24	-4
Tennessee	Inputs	242	169	204	251	195	-47	-19
	Solid, primary	223	219	158	152	104	-119	-53
	Panel	23	35	20	18	9	-14	-61
	Pulp and paper	779	880	755	943	767	-12	-2
	Solid, secondary	721	813	739	836	507	-213	-30
	Pulp and paper products	808	857	763	750	644	-163	-20
Texas	Inputs	266	239	264	298	240	-25	-10
	Solid, primary	25	248	229	247	186	-39	-17
	Panel	255	279	263	253	201	-54	-21
	Pulp and paper	494	457	525	533	383	-111	-22
	Solid, secondary	1,557	1,934	1,661	1,811	1,240	-318	-20
	Pulp and paper products	1,402	1,473	1,448	1,497	1,120	-282	-20
Virginia	Inputs	184	167	182	203	164	-19	-10
	Solid, primary	259	266	217	231	178	-81	-31
	Panel	136	145	130	130	100	-35	-26
	Pulp and paper	512	559	512	527	461	-51	-10
	Solid, secondary	1,086	1,161	965	1,005	689	-396	-37
	Pulp and paper products	396	404	391	388	317	-79	-20
Total	Inputs	3,156	2,853	3,026	3,225	2,662	-494	-16
	Solid, primary	3,000	3,108	2,575	2,646	2,043	-957	-32
	Panel	1,891	1,929	1,799	1,754	1,282	-609	-32
	Pulp and paper	6,925	7,207	6,795	7,125	6,030	-894	-13
	Solid, secondary	9,329	10,739	9,282	9,464	6,364	-2,965	-32
	Pulp and paper products	7,680	8,038	7,484	7,599	6,390	-1,289	-17

Source: IMpact analysis for PLANning (IMPLAN) V3.0.

Table A.32—Forest sector direct effect in output by State and major forest sector group, 2004–09

State	Forest sector group	Year					Change	Change
		2004	2006	2007	2008	2009		
		- - - - - - - - - - - - - - - *millions of dollars* - - - - - - - - - - - - - - -						*percent*
Alabama	Inputs	$2,719	$2,526	$2,470	$2,134	$1,016	$-1,703	-63
	Solid, primary	2,221	2,200	1,896	1,617	1,121	-1,101	-50
	Panel	713	878	800	759	383	-330	-46
	Pulp and paper	6,944	7,148	7,227	7,603	7,161	216	3
	Solid, secondary	2,943	3,316	3,274	2,758	1,789	-1,154	-39
	Pulp and paper products	1,300	1,422	1,430	1,508	1,256	-44	-3
Arkansas	Inputs	1,996	1,800	1,622	1,647	786	-1,210	-61
	Solid, primary	2,088	2,107	1,606	1,386	1,050	-1,038	-50
	Panel	606	738	673	642	501	-105	-17
	Pulp and paper	2,981	3,025	2,903	3,107	3,115	134	4
	Solid, secondary	1,047	953	1,108	1,004	666	-381	-36
	Pulp and paper products	2,918	2,782	2,880	2,928	2,799	-119	-4
Florida	Inputs	1,793	1,944	1,488	1,480	1,000	-793	-44
	Solid, primary	958	924	784	671	471	-487	-51
	Panel	248	256	250	269	199	-49	-20
	Pulp and paper	1,989	2,004	2,021	2,152	2,114	125	6
	Solid, secondary	4,602	5,295	4,223	3,606	2,130	-2,472	-54
	Pulp and paper products	3,106	3,340	3,195	3,498	3,112	7	0
Georgia	Inputs	3,122	3,232	3,183	2,710	1,409	-1,714	-55
	Solid, primary	1,870	2,063	1,937	1,835	1,361	-509	-27
	Panel	868	1,085	940	816	563	-305	-35
	Pulp and paper	6,419	6,237	5,910	6,380	6,128	-291	-5
	Solid, secondary	3,479	3,865	3,720	3,435	2,154	-1,325	-38
	Pulp and paper products	5,815	5,606	5,372	5,610	4,978	-837	-14
Kentucky	Inputs	671	597	353	525	224	-447	-67
	Solid, primary	1,178	1,198	927	796	536	-642	-54
	Panel	122	150	152	152	75	-47	-39
	Pulp and paper	1,127	1,103	1,114	1,169	1,174	47	4
	Solid, secondary	1,957	2,168	2,248	1,985	1,528	-429	-22
	Pulp and paper products	3,043	2,973	3,360	3,421	3,019	-24	-1
Louisiana	Inputs	1,774	1,667	1,773	1,609	780	-994	-56
	Solid, primary	808	870	827	722	501	-307	-38
	Panel	933	1,122	1,054	993	493	-440	-47
	Pulp and paper	3,882	3,670	3,511	3,503	3,166	-716	-18
	Solid, secondary	444	548	587	533	547	103	23
	Pulp and paper products	1,223	1,247	1,266	1,239	1,140	-84	-7
Mississippi	Inputs	2,261	2,219	2,058	1,886	880	-1,381	-61
	Solid, primary	1,930	1,957	1,626	1,390	975	-955	-49
	Panel	751	1,030	1,006	905	578	-173	-23
	Pulp and paper	1,547	1,566	1,501	1,608	1,539	-8	0
	Solid, secondary	869	1,132	1,252	1,244	761	-108	-12
	Pulp and paper products	1,174	1,034	1,042	1,047	874	-300	-26

continued

Table A.32—Forest sector direct effect in output by State and major forest sector group, 2004–09 (continued)

State	Forest sector group	Year					Change	Change
		2004	2006	2007	2008	2009		
		- - - - - - - - - - - - - - - - millions of dollars - - - - - - - - - - - - - - - -						percent
North Carolina	Inputs	2,114	1,950	1,722	1,706	824	-1,290	-61
	Solid, primary	1,865	1,839	1,636	1,350	968	-897	-48
	Panel	1,292	1,501	1,383	1,125	717	-575	-45
	Pulp and paper	3,652	3,678	3,591	3,685	3,379	-273	-7
	Solid, secondary	5,965	5,858	5,278	4,615	3,226	-2,740	-46
	Pulp and paper products	4,496	4,762	4,960	5,282	4,533	37	1
Oklahoma	Inputs	398	412	320	350	176	-222	-56
	Solid, primary	544	446	396	344	244	-300	-55
	Panel	33	55	57	30	27	-6	-18
	Pulp and paper	555	590	1,283	1,390	1,330	775	139
	Solid, secondary	609	699	654	612	390	-219	-36
	Pulp and paper products	952	869	323	339	276	-676	-71
South Carolina	Inputs	1,683	1,556	1,361	1,299	629	-1,053	-63
	Solid, primary	1,094	1,268	1,106	945	672	-422	-39
	Panel	480	643	677	631	532	51	11
	Pulp and paper	3,247	3,438	3,414	3,596	3,348	101	3
	Solid, secondary	938	1,166	1,175	1,113	689	-249	-27
	Pulp and paper products	3,394	3,564	3,742	4,212	4,069	676	20
Tennessee	Inputs	1,258	994	1,254	1,053	582	-676	-54
	Solid, primary	1,415	1,455	1,207	965	658	-757	-54
	Panel	112	194	100	83	50	-63	-56
	Pulp and paper	4,467	4,928	4,550	5,194	4,935	468	10
	Solid, secondary	2,689	2,992	2,893	2,876	1,749	-940	-35
	Pulp and paper products	4,297	4,346	4,200	4,261	3,737	-560	-13
Texas	Inputs	1,895	1,796	1,976	1,805	960	-934	-49
	Solid, primary	1,454	1,500	1,328	1,230	898	-556	-38
	Panel	958	1,420	1,249	1,041	819	-138	-14
	Pulp and paper	2,715	2,511	2,685	2,804	2,539	-176	-6
	Solid, secondary	5,749	6,794	6,440	6,446	4,330	-1,419	-25
	Pulp and paper products	7,149	6,940	6,819	7,020	6,266	-884	-12
Virginia	Inputs	1,297	1,257	1,126	1,100	499	-798	-62
	Solid, primary	1,689	1,694	1,454	1,308	924	-764	-45
	Panel	566	804	719	661	443	-124	-22
	Pulp and paper	3,318	3,456	3,448	3,624	3,392	73	2
	Solid, secondary	4,099	4,108	3,832	3,614	2,336	-1,763	-43
	Pulp and paper products	2,017	1,992	2,082	2,094	1,700	-317	-16
Total	Inputs	22,981	21,950	20,708	19,306	9,764	-13,217	-58
	Solid, primary	19,114	19,520	16,731	14,559	10,379	-8,735	-46
	Panel	7,682	9,877	9,061	8,104	5,378	-2,304	-30
	Pulp and paper	42,844	43,352	43,158	45,814	43,319	476	1
	Solid, secondary	35,391	38,894	36,686	33,842	22,296	-13,095	-37
	Pulp and paper products	40,885	40,876	40,670	42,459	37,758	-3,126	-8

Source: IMpact analysis for PLANning (IMPLAN) V3.0.

Table A.33—Forest sector total effect in employment by State and major forest sector group, 2004–09

State	Forest sector group	2004	2006	2007	2008	2009	Change	Change
				Year				
		------------ number of jobs (full- and part-time) ------------						*percent*
Alabama	Inputs	19,103	18,597	14,144	14,815	11,203	-7,900	-41
	Solid, primary	13,461	13,524	11,348	10,654	8,826	-4,635	-34
	Panel	5,664	5,915	5,530	5,238	2,955	-2,709	-48
	Pulp and paper	36,044	33,009	37,523	33,987	35,696	-348	-1
	Solid, secondary	29,800	34,066	36,413	32,878	22,150	-7,650	-26
	Pulp and paper products	8,479	8,661	9,096	9,016	7,836	-643	-8
Arkansas	Inputs	16,303	16,064	10,782	12,677	8,624	-7,679	-47
	Solid, primary	12,688	12,883	9,380	9,000	7,659	-5,029	-40
	Panel	4,819	5,145	4,471	4,311	3,603	-1,216	-25
	Pulp and paper	15,748	14,632	14,550	13,672	14,001	-1,747	-11
	Solid, secondary	10,996	10,189	11,416	11,105	7,290	-3,706	-34
	Pulp and paper products	17,551	16,252	15,195	14,354	13,310	-4,240	-24
Florida	Inputs	25,975	30,719	16,963	24,870	18,864	-7,111	-27
	Solid, primary	6,089	5,868	5,316	5,013	4,197	-1,892	-31
	Panel	2,113	2,051	2,073	2,167	2,010	-103	-5
	Pulp and paper	11,288	10,157	13,632	12,517	13,499	2,211	20
	Solid, secondary	46,443	53,620	51,097	45,578	27,936	-18,506	-40
	Pulp and paper products	20,374	20,314	22,006	21,988	19,836	-537	-3
Georgia	Inputs	23,565	27,521	20,512	21,992	15,684	-7,882	-33
	Solid, primary	11,340	12,571	12,379	12,906	11,419	79	1
	Panel	6,825	6,942	6,457	5,716	4,428	-2,397	-35
	Pulp and paper	34,946	30,619	35,237	33,009	35,710	764	2
	Solid, secondary	34,810	39,171	42,531	40,023	26,330	-8,480	-24
	Pulp and paper products	38,035	34,646	34,157	32,676	29,859	-8,177	-21
Kentucky	Inputs	5,566	4,879	3,633	4,900	3,071	-2,495	-45
	Solid, primary	7,870	8,087	5,538	5,226	4,167	-3,703	-47
	Panel	1,033	1,235	1,181	1,130	707	-326	-32
	Pulp and paper	5,713	5,169	5,646	5,104	5,579	-135	-2
	Solid, secondary	19,254	21,049	22,515	20,632	15,876	-3,378	-18
	Pulp and paper products	19,248	17,931	19,190	18,271	16,739	-2,509	-13
Louisiana	Inputs	12,470	12,677	10,720	12,455	8,855	-3,614	-29
	Solid, primary	4,784	5,111	4,825	4,692	3,673	-1,111	-23
	Panel	7,664	7,907	7,269	6,804	3,489	-4,175	-54
	Pulp and paper	21,503	17,685	18,410	16,240	14,732	-6,771	-31
	Solid, secondary	4,807	5,865	6,310	6,012	5,910	1,103	23
	Pulp and paper products	8,265	7,854	7,823	7,608	6,932	-1,333	-16
Mississippi	Inputs	17,312	17,010	13,208	14,091	9,702	-7,610	-44
	Solid, primary	11,202	11,479	9,344	8,958	7,167	-4,035	-36
	Panel	5,615	6,147	6,101	5,828	3,935	-1,680	-30
	Pulp and paper	7,506	6,863	7,137	6,861	6,721	-785	-10
	Solid, secondary	9,141	11,605	13,069	13,169	8,216	-925	-10
	Pulp and paper products	7,178	6,145	6,089	5,855	4,839	-2,339	-33

continued

Table A.33—Forest sector total effect in employment by State and major forest sector group, 2004–09 (continued)

State	Forest sector group	Year					Change	Change
		2004	2006	2007	2008	2009		
		- - - - - - - - - - - - - *number of jobs (full- and part-time)* - - - - - - - - - - - - -						*percent*
North Carolina	Inputs	15,097	15,532	12,605	15,074	10,503	-4,594	-30
	Solid, primary	11,598	11,386	10,252	9,269	7,825	-3,773	-33
	Panel	10,407	9,967	9,583	8,034	5,681	-4,726	-45
	Pulp and paper	19,065	17,265	20,459	18,045	18,059	-1,006	-5
	Solid, secondary	59,331	58,850	60,568	53,624	36,799	-22,532	-38
	Pulp and paper products	29,159	29,182	33,123	32,995	29,143	-16	0
Oklahoma	Inputs	4,781	5,649	2,206	2,628	1,816	-2,965	-62
	Solid, primary	3,317	2,622	2,293	2,182	1,761	-1,556	-47
	Panel	310	373	355	202	181	-129	-42
	Pulp and paper	3,384	3,152	6,783	6,321	6,580	3,197	94
	Solid, secondary	6,507	7,601	7,172	7,078	4,670	-1,837	-28
	Pulp and paper products	6,495	5,266	2,069	2,068	1,750	-4,745	-73
South Carolina	Inputs	11,290	11,657	9,077	10,611	7,613	-3,676	-33
	Solid, primary	6,164	7,126	6,723	6,321	5,360	-804	-13
	Panel	3,655	3,713	4,121	4,047	3,480	-175	-5
	Pulp and paper	15,864	15,080	18,635	17,132	17,534	1,669	11
	Solid, secondary	9,609	11,545	12,417	12,713	8,381	-1,228	-13
	Pulp and paper products	20,414	20,367	21,931	21,729	21,766	1,352	7
Tennessee	Inputs	7,401	6,589	7,087	7,231	6,577	-824	-11
	Solid, primary	9,434	9,792	7,600	6,671	5,516	-3,918	-42
	Panel	991	1,209	691	584	288	-703	-71
	Pulp and paper	24,370	24,470	25,289	24,908	26,349	1,979	8
	Solid, secondary	7,391	30,954	31,324	31,720	21,038	-6,353	-23
	Pulp and paper products	29,084	28,223	26,709	25,921	24,160	-4,924	-17
Texas	Inputs	16,452	16,016	13,908	17,186	12,212	-4,240	-26
	Solid, primary	8,961	9,199	8,174	8,422	7,563	-1,398	-16
	Panel	7,340	8,263	8,003	6,975	6,349	-991	-13
	Pulp and paper	14,732	12,166	15,753	14,592	15,244	511	3
	Solid, secondary	59,173	70,839	75,252	76,272	56,181	-2,992	-5
	Pulp and paper products	45,680	42,064	44,297	43,106	40,933	-4,747	-10
Virginia	Inputs	7,269	7,402	7,056	7,732	5,671	-1,598	-22
	Solid, primary	10,214	10,471	8,560	8,488	6,979	-3,235	-32
	Panel	4,184	4,932	4,557	4,363	3,137	-1,047	-25
	Pulp and paper	16,330	15,505	17,909	16,438	16,336	6	0
	Solid, secondary	39,765	41,168	39,928	38,280	25,756	-14,008	-35
	Pulp and paper products	12,981	12,305	13,295	12,823	10,585	-2,396	-18
Total	Inputs	182,583	190,312	141,902	166,263	120,395	-62,188	-34
	Solid, primary	117,122	120,119	101,731	97,802	82,113	-35,010	-30
	Panel	60,619	63,798	60,393	55,399	40,243	-20,376	-34
	Pulp and paper	226,493	205,772	236,963	218,827	226,040	-453	0
	Solid, secondary	357,028	396,523	410,012	389,086	266,535	-90,493	-25
	Pulp and paper products	262,943	249,211	254,979	248,409	227,689	-35,253	-13

Source: IMpact analysis for PLANning (IMPLAN) V3.0.

Table A. 34—Forest sector total effect in labor income by State and major forest sector group, 2004–09

State	Forest sector group	Year					Change	Change
		2004	2006	2007	2008	2009		
				- - - - - - - - - - millions of dollars - - - - - - - - - - -				percent
Alabama	Inputs	$774	$716	$585	$624	$484	$-289	-37
	Solid, primary	584	588	498	471	382	-202	-35
	Panel	268	275	258	245	138	-130	-49
	Pulp and paper	2,270	2,262	2,431	2,312	2,140	-130	-6
	Solid, secondary	1,125	1,372	1,385	1,234	835	-290	-26
	Pulp and paper products	441	483	498	507	415	-26	-6
Arkansas	Inputs	585	531	388	470	326	-259	-44
	Solid, primary	513	526	390	388	332	-181	-35
	Panel	216	225	207	204	186	-29	-14
	Pulp and paper	887	875	825	815	839	-48	-5
	Solid, secondary	388	374	409	403	279	-108	-28
	Pulp and paper products	829	802	746	725	690	-139	-17
Florida	Inputs	773	888	532	759	592	-181	-23
	Solid, primary	280	272	243	218	184	-96	-34
	Panel	102	98	99	106	99	-2	-2
	Pulp and paper	716	681	851	805	811	95	13
	Solid, secondary	2,013	2,487	2,261	2,004	1,244	-769	-38
	Pulp and paper products	1,158	1,226	1,274	1,281	1,119	-39	-3
Georgia	Inputs	910	1,002	840	890	683	-227	-25
	Solid, primary	526	585	573	595	540	13	3
	Panel	370	370	330	290	231	-139	-38
	Pulp and paper	2,302	2,133	2,293	2,210	2,219	-83	-4
	Solid, secondary	1,491	1,741	1,867	1,721	1,153	-338	-23
	Pulp and paper products	2,206	2,081	2,032	1,942	1,732	-474	-21
Kentucky	Inputs	160	129	88	144	82	-77	-49
	Solid, primary	276	285	193	188	147	-129	-47
	Panel	36	45	43	43	26	-11	-30
	Pulp and paper	342	320	329	323	332	-10	-3
	Solid, secondary	787	923	924	857	674	-113	-14
	Pulp and paper products	1,025	983	1,020	1,008	890	-135	-13
Louisiana	Inputs	484	457	442	521	384	-100	-21
	Solid, primary	211	228	220	224	180	-31	-15
	Panel	361	369	352	342	182	-179	-50
	Pulp and paper	1,246	1,113	1,152	1,085	967	-280	-22
	Solid, secondary	172	229	247	240	254	82	48
	Pulp and paper products	429	425	419	429	377	-52	-12
Mississippi	Inputs	633	602	486	536	392	-241	-38
	Solid, primary	467	483	390	376	306	-161	-34
	Panel	270	282	282	269	188	-82	-30
	Pulp and paper	465	458	455	454	420	-45	-10
	Solid, secondary	314	439	472	484	313	-1	0
	Pulp and paper products	366	326	320	318	242	-124	-34

continued

Table A. 34—Forest sector total effect in labor income by State and major forest sector group, 2004–09 (continued)

State	Forest sector group	Year 2004	2006	2007	2008	2009	Change	Change
		- - - - - - - - - - - - - - - - - *millions of dollars* - - - - - - - - - - - - - - - - -						*percent*
North Carolina	Inputs	565	528	455	564	407	-158	-28
	Solid, primary	488	478	438	398	336	-152	-31
	Panel	462	446	431	370	270	-192	-42
	Pulp and paper	1,132	1,092	1,204	1,118	1,057	-75	-7
	Solid, secondary	2,439	2,594	2,519	2,233	1,589	-850	-35
	Pulp and paper products	1,588	1,654	1,795	1,838	1,570	-18	-1
Oklahoma	Inputs	140	144	69	92	59	-81	-58
	Solid, primary	161	130	117	122	99	-62	-39
	Panel	11	13	13	8	7	-4	-36
	Pulp and paper	178	182	379	374	377	199	112
	Solid, secondary	240	285	262	263	178	-62	-26
	Pulp and paper products	330	301	102	107	89	-241	-73
South Carolina	Inputs	415	402	339	392	301	-114	-27
	Solid, primary	265	330		281	235	-30	-11
	Panel	163	171	194	196	173	9	6
	Pulp and paper	966	1,015	1,113	1,058	995	29	3
	Solid, secondary	352	469	497	498	331	-21	-6
	Pulp and paper products	1,153	1,233	1,264	1,260	1,204	51	4
Tennessee	Inputs	394	292	328	396	321	-73	-18
	Solid, primary	398	404	306	275	217	-181	-45
	Panel	40	60	33	29	15	-25	-63
	Pulp and paper	1,617	1,727	1,673	1,849	1,746	129	8
	Solid, secondary	1,180	1,380	1,362	1,428	910	-270	-23
	Pulp and paper products	1,594	1,631	1,519	1,481	1,313	-282	-18
Texas	Inputs	638	600	574	725	515	-123	-19
	Solid, primary	417	450	417	428	365	-52	-12
	Panel	408	472	472	423	353	-55	-14
	Pulp and paper	1,063	938	1,219	1,166	1,027	-37	-3
	Solid, secondary	2,541	3,248	3,362	3,418	2,464	-77	-3
	Pulp and paper products	2,762	2,743	2,916	2,920	2,443	-320	-12
Virginia	Inputs	299	280	276	326	247	-52	-17
	Solid, primary	442	458	389	389	326	-116	-26
	Panel	208	234	221	211	160	-48	-23
	Pulp and paper	1,068	1,091	1,218	1,160	1,112	44	4
	Solid, secondary	1,690	1,858	1,765	1,701	1,189	-501	-30
	Pulp and paper products	724	721	775	754	619	-105	-15
Total	Inputs	6,768	6,570	5,400	6,439	4,792	-1,976	-29
	Solid, primary	5,029	5,214	4,461	4,351	3,649	-1,380	-27
	Panel	2,915	3,061	2,936	2,736	2,028	-887	-30
	Pulp and paper	14,253	13,885	15,143	14,731	14,041	-213	-1
	Solid, secondary	14,731	17,398	17,331	16,486	11,414	-3,317	-23
	Pulp and paper products	14,605	14,608	14,679	14,569	12,702	-1,903	-13

Source: IMpact analysis for PLANning (IMPLAN) V3.0.

Table A.35—Forest sector total effect in output by State and major forest sector group, 2004–09

State	Forest sector group	Year					Change	Change
		2004	2006	2007	2008	2009		
		- - - - - - - - - - - - - - - - - - *millions of dollars* - - - - - - - - - - - - - - - - - -						*percent*
Alabama	Inputs	$3,641	$3,393	$3,013	$2,755	$1,443	$-2,198	-60
	Solid, primary	2,917	2,918	2,477	2,126	1,576	-1,341	-46
	Panel	997	1,195	1,081	1,017	531	-466	-47
	Pulp and paper	10,687	10,722	11,176	11,178	10,835	148	1
	Solid, secondary	4,123	4,869	5,096	4,233	2,783	-1,340	-33
	Pulp and paper products	1,863	2,035	2,072	2,148	1,788	-75	-4
Arkansas	Inputs	2,801	2,580	2,002	2,177	1,088	-1,713	-61
	Solid, primary	2,699	2,761	2,054	1,799	1,421	-1,279	-47
	Panel	834	1,005	881	841	667	-168	-20
	Pulp and paper	4,571	4,604	4,309	4,434	4,494	-77	-2
	Solid, secondary	1,481	1,403	1,621	1,464	968	-513	-35
	Pulp and paper products	4,222	4,054	3,944	3,950	3,713	-509	-12
Florida	Inputs	3,109	3,379	2,243	2,691	1,908	-1,201	-39
	Solid, primary	1,334	1,300	1,140	982	749	-586	-44
	Panel	368	378	380	402	322	-46	-12
	Pulp and paper	3,178	3,113	3,625	3,623	3,680	503	16
	Solid, secondary	6,910	8,330	7,758	6,541	3,913	-2,997	-43
	Pulp and paper products	4,887	5,201	5,331	5,620	4,962	75	2
Georgia	Inputs	4,353	4,597	4,197	3,871	2,199	-2,154	-49
	Solid, primary	2,557	2,857	2,750	2,621	2,111	-446	-17
	Panel	1,291	1,549	1,374	1,173	836	-455	-35
	Pulp and paper	10,453	9,873	10,180	10,303	10,326	-126	-1
	Solid, secondary	5,231	6,079	6,525	5,872	3,735	-1,496	-29
	Pulp and paper products	9,390	8,864	8,598	8,650	7,622	-1,768	-19
Kentucky	Inputs	913	802	436	713	315	-598	-66
	Solid, primary	1,532	1,577	1,183	1,030	737	-795	-52
	Panel	170	211	200	200	105	-66	-39
	Pulp and paper	1,723	1,673	1,688	1,711	1,752	29	2
	Solid, secondary	2,807	3,212	3,335	2,928	2,266	-541	-19
	Pulp and paper products	4,588	4,466	4,764	4,813	4,224	-364	-8
Louisiana	Inputs	2,424	2,315	2,251	2,241	1,176	-1,248	-51
	Solid, primary	1,070	1,157	1,092	975	704	-366	-34
	Panel	1,337	1,568	1,457	1,390	700	-637	-48
	Pulp and paper	6,232	5,727	5,668	5,508	4,892	-1,340	-21
	Solid, secondary	643	818	914	833	829	186	29
	Pulp and paper products	1,818	1,833	1,860	1,850	1,649	-169	-9
Mississippi	Inputs	3,111	3,062	2,528	2,457	1,237	-1,874	-60
	Solid, primary	2,452	2,529	2,058	1,783	1,318	-1,134	-46
	Panel	1,031	1,378	1,310	1,185	759	-272	-26
	Pulp and paper	2,297	2,294	2,172	2,260	2,194	-103	-4
	Solid, secondary	1,203	1,630	1,802	1,774	1,091	-112	-9
	Pulp and paper products	1,659	1,467	1,428	1,429	1,172	-487	-29

continued

Table A.35—Forest sector total effect in output by State and major forest sector group, 2004–09 (continued)

State	Forest sector group	Year					Change	Change
		2004	2006	2007	2008	2009		
		----------------- millions of dollars -----------------						percent
North Carolina	Inputs	2,852	2,663	2,230	2,441	1,284	-1,568	-55
	Solid, primary	2,457	2,445	2,215	1,840	1,407	-1,050	-43
	Panel	1,824	2,053	1,919	1,547	1,015	-809	-44
	Pulp and paper	5,631	5,536	5,734	5,577	5,249	-382	-7
	Solid, secondary	8,575	8,905	8,753	7,466	5,177	-3,398	-40
	Pulp and paper products	6,678	7,068	7,608	7,934	6,741	63	1
Oklahoma	Inputs	644	683	396	476	245	-399	-62
	Solid, primary	737	608	524	466	347	-390	-53
	Panel	49	77	78	41	35	-15	-29
	Pulp and paper	918	948	2,034	2,107	2,065	1,147	125
	Solid, secondary	893	1,075	1,015	952	605	-289	-32
	Pulp and paper products	1,495	1,348	467	491	395	-1,100	-74
South Carolina	Inputs	2,167	2,034	1,699	1,745	920	-1,247	-58
	Solid, primary	1,403	1,647	1,457	1,260	957	-445	-32
	Panel	654	840	910	852	716	63	10
	Pulp and paper	4,806	4,943	5,257	5,302	5,059	253	5
	Solid, secondary	1,315	1,683	1,807	1,703	1,081	-234	-18
	Pulp and paper products	4,889	5,122	5,413	5,908	5,680	791	16
Tennessee	Inputs	1,693	1,347	1,602	1,466	917	-776	-46
	Solid, primary	1,942	2,024	1,639	1,335	985	-957	-49
	Panel	165	274	141	118	68	-97	-59
	Pulp and paper	7,177	7,754	7,365	8,104	7,962	785	11
	Solid, secondary	4,094	4,769	4,758	4,684	2,923	-1,171	-29
	Pulp and paper products	6,732	6,822	6,444	6,481	5,690	-1,042	-15
Texas	Inputs	2,856	2,728	2,744	2,861	1,660	-1,196	-42
	Solid, primary	2,050	2,152	1,910	1,799	1,441	-608	-30
	Panel	1,458	2,098	1,961	1,659	1,344	-115	-8
	Pulp and paper	4,686	4,279	4,980	4,996	4,716	30	1
	Solid, secondary	8,793	11,037	11,804	11,639	8,085	-709	-8
	Pulp and paper products	11,527	11,223	11,488	11,784	10,627	-900	-8
Virginia	Inputs	1,624	1,578	1,390	1,447	724	-900	-55
	Solid, primary	2,233	2,278	1,958	1,781	1,346	-887	-40
	Panel	788	1,085	994	913	619	-169	-21
	Pulp and paper	5,074	5,172	5,595	5,620	5,346	272	5
	Solid, secondary	5,917	6,252	6,191	5,738	3,771	-2,145	-36
	Pulp and paper products	2,997	2,963	3,206	3,192	2,563	-435	-14
Total	Inputs	32,188	31,160	26,731	27,339	15,117	-17,071	-53
	Solid, primary	25,383	26,253	22,456	19,796	15,100	-10,283	-41
	Panel	10,968	13,713	12,687	11,337	7,716	-3,252	-30
	Pulp and paper	67,432	66,638	69,784	70,722	68,571	1,139	2
	Solid, secondary	51,985	60,063	61,381	55,827	37,226	-14,759	-28
	Pulp and paper products	62,746	62,464	62,623	64,248	56,826	-5,920	-9

Source: IMpact analysis for PLANning (IMPLAN) V3.0.

Table A.36—Area of timberland by State, survey year, stand origin, and stand treatment, 1980s periodic inventories

State	Survey year	Total timberland	Stand origin		Stand treatment		
			Natural stands	Planted stands	Clearcut	Partial harvest[a]	Other[b]
			- thousand acres -				
Alabama	1990	21,932.0	17,520.8	4,411.2	2,640.1	3,784.4	1,602.6
Arkansas	1988	17,244.8	15,434.9	1,809.8	1,407.5	4,341.7	865.2
Florida	1987	14,984.6	10,763.6	4,221.1	2,288.6	284.6	401.4
Georgia	1989	23,636.0	18,132.4	5,503.6	3,970.0	946.9	583.8
Kentucky	1988	12,347.8	12,191.2	156.5	—	—	—
Louisiana	1984	13,872.6	11,907.7	1,964.9	1,341.8	2,711.8	1,679.1
Mississippi	1987	16,986.6	14,198.8	2,787.8	2,083.9	4,128.3	1,231.7
North Carolina	1984	18,449.4	16,717.8	1,731.6	2,521.4	588.1	422.0
Oklahoma (east)	1986	4,741.2	4,216.7	524.5	458.6	658.8	154.6
South Carolina	1986	12,184.7	10,011.9	2,172.8	2,140.8	498.2	586.3
Tennessee	1989	13,265.2	12,746.8	518.4	416.9	2,135.3	143.8
Texas (east)	1986	11,571.1	9,772.0	1,799.1	1,636.7	3,246.2	22.1
Virginia	1985	15,436.9	13,926.9	1,510.0	1,694.6	307.6	192.9
Total		196,652.9	167,541.6	29,111.4	22,601.0	23,631.9	7,885.4

— = no sample for the cell.

[a] Partial harvest includes all conditions recorded as having either partial harvest or seed tree/shelterwood.

[b] Includes commercial thinnings, timber stand improvement, and salvage cuttings.

Table A.37—Area of timberland by State, survey year, stand origin, and stand treatment, 1990s periodic inventories

State	Survey year	Total timberland	Stand origin		Stand treatment		
			Natural stands	Planted stands	Clearcut	Partial harvest[a]	Other[b]
			- thousand acres -				
Alabama	2000	22,675.9	16,887.4	5,788.5	3,978.3	2,010.2	1,359.6
Arkansas	1995	18,391.8	15,975.0	2,410.6	735.5	3,162.7	1,225.8
Florida	1995	14,653.8	9,707.5	4,946.3	1,797.7	154.1	330.9
Georgia	1997	24,593.0	17,547.6	7,045.4	3,894.9	878.9	904.4
Kentucky	1988	12,347.8	12,191.2	156.5	—	—	—
Louisiana	1991	13,783.0	11,136.2	2,646.8	1,440.7	2,932.7	1,319.6
Mississippi	1994	18,587.3	14,475.7	4,111.6	1,904.6	3,716.2	1,085.9
North Carolina	1990	18,710.3	16,421.7	2,288.6	1,837.3	328.0	385.9
Oklahoma (east)	1993	4,895.5	4,285.3	610.2	98.9	527.3	196.3
South Carolina	2001	12,725.0	9,326.5	3,398.5	1,526.2	672.2	679.7
Tennessee	1999	13,305.2	12,702.8	602.5	499.2	1,409.0	82.3
Texas (east)	1992	11,773.8	9,360.1	2,413.7	1,022.5	2,349.6	589.4
Virginia	2001	15,486.1	13,370.5	2,115.6	1,270.4	908.0	305.2
Total		201,928.6	163,387.5	38,535.0	20,006.3	19,049.0	8,464.9

— = no sample for the cell.

[a] Partial harvest includes all conditions recorded as having either partial harvest or seed tree/shelterwood.

[b] Includes commercial thinnings, timber stand improvement, and salvage cuttings.

Table A.38—Area of timberland by State, survey year, stand origin, and stand treatment, 2005 moving average inventory

| State | Survey year | Total timberland | Stand origin | | Stand treatment | | |
			Natural stands	Planted stands	Clearcut	Partial harvest[a]	Other[b]
					- - - - - - - - thousand acres - - - - - - - -		
Alabama	2006	22,687.8	16,157.7	6,530.1	1,721.7	721.2	1,243.4
Arkansas	2005	17,996.2	15,063.4	2,932.8	1,230.9	2,056.8	1,134.7
Florida	2007	15,912.1	10,682.3	5,229.9	1,885.6	713.0	678.7
Georgia	2006	24,522.8	16,820.3	7,702.5	1,696.9	835.3	1,373.3
Kentucky	2007	12,111.9	12,020.8	91.1	77.8	1,204.7	69.1
Louisiana	2005	14,238.4	9,932.8	4,305.6	2,332.2	1,598.4	1,452.3
Mississippi	2006	19,557.0	14,002.3	5,554.7	3,315.6	1,939.0	1,708.7
North Carolina	2007	18,050.4	14,788.0	3,262.4	1,149.5	383.7	607.7
Oklahoma (east)	2008	5,103.1	4,425.4	677.7	499.3	629.2	279.1
South Carolina	2006	12,985.5	9,486.8	3,498.6	718.8	338.4	796.6
Tennessee	2006	13,400.5	12,791.2	609.3	381.1	940.5	30.4
Texas (east)	2006	11,898.3	9,020.4	2,877.9	1,011.5	887.1	802.2
Virginia	2006	15,309.7	12,991.9	2,317.8	843.5	575.5	305.7
Total		203,773.7	158,183.4	45,590.3	16,864.4	12,822.8	10,482.1

[a] Partial harvest includes all conditions recorded as having either partial harvest or seed tree/shelterwood.

[b] Includes commercial thinnings, timber stand improvement, and salvage cuttings.

Table A.39—Area of timberland by State, survey year, stand origin, and stand treatment, 2010 moving average inventory

| State | Survey year | Total timberland | Stand origin | | Stand treatment | | |
			Natural stands	Planted stands	Clearcut	Partial harvest[a]	Other[b]
					- - - - - - - - thousand acres - - - - - - - -		
Alabama	2010	22,738.0	15,828.5	6,909.5	1,994.3	1,033.4	1,581.1
Arkansas	2010	18,521.5	15,259.6	3,261.9	1,008.1	935.4	1,376.5
Florida	2010	15,993.5	10,991.6	5,001.9	1,586.6	628.0	827.1
Georgia	2010	24,395.1	16,645.2	7,749.8	1,506.8	664.3	2,174.7
Kentucky	2010	12,218.0	12,166.3	51.7	75.0	957.0	65.4
Louisiana	2010	14,472.8	10,067.5	4,405.3	2,106.9	1,350.5	1,532.5
Mississippi	2010	19,519.5	13,878.5	5,641.1	2,565.4	1,406.8	1,476.6
North Carolina	2010	18,107.5	14,878.9	3,228.6	1,120.8	368.6	550.9
Oklahoma (east)	2010	7,747.5	7,077.6	669.9	426.7	470.3	275.4
South Carolina	2010	13,004.1	9,611.3	3,392.8	702.9	279.2	1,255.8
Tennessee	2010	13,544.7	12,856.0	688.8	325.3	661.9	47.1
Texas (east)	2010	11,979.6	8,937.2	3,042.4	782.6	636.1	945.5
Virginia	2010	15,412.0	12,941.3	2,470.7	554.2	440.9	278.5
Total		207,653.8	161,139.5	46,514.3	14,755.5	9,832.5	12,387.1

[a] Partial harvest includes all conditions recorded as having either partial harvest or seed tree/shelterwood.

[b] Includes commercial thinnings, timber stand improvement, and salvage cuttings.

Table A.40—Current volume, average annual growth, average annual removals, and average annual saw-log removals of all-live trees on timberland by State and survey year, 1980s periodic inventories

State	Survey year	Volume			Average annual growth			Average annual removals			Average annual saw-log removals		
		Total	Soft-wood	Hard-wood	Total	Soft-wood	Hard-wood	Total	Soft-wood	Hard-wood	Total	Soft-wood	Hard-wood
		- *million cubic feet* -											
Alabama	1990	24,735.9	11,293.1	13,442.8	1,211.6	650.8	560.8	1,116.8	726.1	390.6	801.7	564.0	237.7
Arkansas	1988	20,761.1	8,085.1	12,676.0	767.7	377.9	389.8	689.7	409.4	280.3	526.8	343.4	183.4
Florida	1987	17,427.1	9,438.7	7,988.4	654.4	488.9	165.4	562.0	476.5	85.5	323.1	274.3	48.8
Georgia	1989	32,612.9	15,679.9	16,932.9	1,293.8	818.7	475.1	1,337.1	961.8	375.3	931.5	689.7	241.7
Kentucky	1988	16,578.9	1,237.9	15,341.0	—	—	—	—	—	—	—	—	—
Louisiana	1984	21,614.9	11,087.9	10,526.9	876.6	579.1	297.6	693.0	450.4	242.6	539.5	368.6	170.9
Mississippi	1987	22,361.9	9,473.7	12,888.2	986.8	485.6	501.2	754.9	485.5	269.4	569.4	385.2	184.2
North Carolina	1984	30,854.8	11,326.6	19,528.2	1,145.2	502.0	643.2	789.4	433.4	356.0	587.0	344.6	242.5
Oklahoma (east)	1986	3,083.9	1,059.8	2,024.0	98.9	49.4	49.6	101.1	57.3	43.8	68.7	43.4	25.2
South Carolina	1986	19,199.4	8,930.0	10,269.3	705.8	446.9	258.9	660.0	464.5	195.5	480.7	352.8	127.9
Tennessee	1989	18,259.3	2,967.6	15,291.7	566.3	99.2	467.1	257.7	54.1	203.6	196.7	36.1	160.5
Texas (east)	1986	14,125.8	8,014.1	6,111.7	603.6	415.3	188.2	588.9	431.5	157.4	461.0	360.0	101.0
Virginia	1985	25,338.1	5,990.8	19,347.3	816.7	227.9	588.8	519.5	209.0	310.5	370.2	150.2	220.0
Total		266,953.8	104,585.3	162,368.5	9,727.4	5,141.8	4,585.6	8,070.0	5,159.3	2,910.7	5,856.3	3,912.3	1,944.0

— = no sample for the cell.

Table A.41—Current volume, average annual growth, average annual removals, and average annual saw-log removals of all-live trees on timberland by State and survey year, 1990s periodic inventories

State	Survey year	Volume			Average annual growth			Average annual removals			Average annual saw-log removals		
		Total	Soft-wood	Hard-wood	Total	Soft-wood	Hard-wood	Total	Soft-wood	Hard-wood	Total	Soft-wood	Hard-wood
		- *million cubic feet* -											
Alabama	2000	30,891.6	13,345.9	17,545.7	1,613.1	923.4	689.6	1,378.6	913.9	464.7	924.2	652.8	271.4
Arkansas	1995	23,758.9	9,534.3	14,224.6	951.7	554.6	397.1	743.7	433.1	310.6	565.1	349.9	215.1
Florida	1995	17,584.3	9,525.7	8,058.6	715.1	532.3	182.8	583.6	475.0	108.6	336.1	269.1	67.0
Georgia	1997	35,201.7	16,470.5	18,731.3	1,578.2	1,032.7	545.4	1,526.5	1,092.1	434.4	1,058.7	790.0	268.7
Kentucky	1988	16,578.9	1,237.9	15,341.0	—	—	—	—	—	—	—	—	—
Louisiana	1991	20,735.4	10,122.4	10,613.0	850.3	524.6	325.8	954.7	669.0	285.6	740.3	544.6	195.7
Mississippi	1994	22,650.2	9,363.5	13,286.7	1,100.8	638.0	462.8	1,211.3	715.9	495.4	927.9	580.0	348.0
North Carolina	1990	34,680.9	12,607.0	22,074.0	1,177.1	591.0	586.1	973.9	513.1	460.7	734.5	402.8	331.7
Oklahoma (east)	1993	3,913.3	1,431.1	2,482.2	203.9	114.9	89.1	88.3	55.5	32.8	58.7	40.6	18.1
South Carolina	2001	20,349.4	9,836.2	10,513.2	990.9	686.5	304.4	765.0	514.3	250.7	548.1	386.4	161.7
Tennessee	1999	25,029.9	3,791.6	21,238.3	845.4	152.7	692.7	411.2	106.5	304.7	324.7	79.2	245.5
Texas (east)	1992	14,229.7	8,008.8	6,221.0	701.2	508.3	192.9	688.4	515.1	173.3	542.1	433.4	108.8
Virginia	2001	30,560.6	6,941.5	23,619.1	990.3	326.8	663.5	698.0	298.7	399.2	500.5	203.4	297.1
Total		296,164.8	112,216.3	183,948.5	11,718.0	6,585.7	5,132.3	10,023.1	6,302.3	3,720.9	7,260.9	4,732.1	2,528.8

— = no sample for the cell.

Table A.42—Current volume, average annual growth, average annual removals, and average annual saw-log removals of all-live trees on timberland by State and survey year, 2005 moving average inventory

State	Survey year	Volume			Average annual growth			Average annual removals			Average annual saw-log removals		
		Total	Soft-wood	Hard-wood	Total	Soft-wood	Hard-wood	Total	Soft-wood	Hard-wood	Total	Soft-wood	Hard-wood
		-- million cubic feet ---											
Alabama	2006	32,617.4	14,512.9	18,104.5	1,666.9	1,045.6	621.3	1,193.1	794.0	399.1	787.1	538.0	249.1
Arkansas	2005	27,215.4	10,357.2	16,858.2	1,100.6	602.0	498.6	906.8	559.5	347.3	670.8	436.3	234.5
Florida	2007	19,342.3	10,967.9	8,374.4	743.5	567.2	176.2	563.6	444.1	119.5	311.1	242.5	68.6
Georgia	2006	38,150.8	18,774.8	19,376.0	1,922.4	1,371.7	550.7	1,425.5	1,053.7	371.8	921.3	680.8	240.5
Kentucky	2007	22,910.1	1,496.2	21,413.9	777.9	48.9	729.1	369.9	29.6	340.3	317.7	25.6	292.1
Louisiana	2005	22,729.7	10,713.8	12,015.9	859.1	577.1	282.0	995.6	667.2	328.3	773.4	541.4	232.0
Mississippi	2006	29,568.2	13,152.6	16,415.7	1,380.9	831.8	549.1	1,076.4	626.2	450.2	759.2	446.6	312.6
North Carolina	2007	35,810.3	12,349.5	23,460.7	1,462.6	710.7	751.8	1,148.0	612.9	535.1	868.2	491.4	376.8
Oklahoma (east)	2008	5,143.5	1,638.9	3,504.6	175.8	93.5	82.4	128.8	71.2	57.6	78.7	47.1	31.6
South Carolina	2006	21,762.8	10,761.5	11,001.4	1,148.8	771.5	377.3	753.5	544.5	209.1	525.4	394.1	131.3
Tennessee	2006	26,643.3	3,103.9	23,539.5	804.0	32.6	771.4	538.4	137.5	400.9	431.9	105.1	326.7
Texas (east)	2006	17,211.1	9,390.9	7,820.2	1,070.6	678.0	392.6	742.7	548.3	194.4	530.1	403.4	126.7
Virginia	2006	31,396.9	7,250.0	24,146.9	974.4	383.3	591.2	827.0	351.8	475.2	586.5	232.3	354.1
Total		330,501.8	124,470.0	206,031.8	14,087.4	7,713.7	6,373.7	10,669.2	6,440.6	4,228.6	7,561.5	4,584.8	2,976.7

Table A.43—Current volume, average annual growth, average annual removals, and average annual saw-log removals of all-live trees on timberland by State and survey year, 2010 moving average inventory

State	Survey year	Volume			Average annual growth			Average annual removals			Average annual saw-log removals		
		Total	Soft-wood	Hard-wood	Total	Soft-wood	Hard-wood	Total	Soft-wood	Hard-wood	Total	Soft-wood	Hard-wood
		-- million cubic feet ---											
Alabama	2010	33,908.0	15,331.7	18,576.3	1,735.4	1,146.3	589.1	1,270.1	900.1	370.1	838.4	610.7	227.7
Arkansas	2010	28,926.5	11,125.1	17,801.4	1,256.8	753.7	503.0	863.2	550.5	312.8	652.9	444.1	208.8
Florida	2010	20,118.3	11,455.1	8,663.2	766.1	530.1	236.0	283.7	234.9	48.8	157.4	128.0	29.4
Georgia	2010	40,432.8	19,989.3	20,443.5	1,922.2	1,379.8	542.4	1,396.7	1,119.0	277.7	849.3	675.4	173.9
Kentucky	2010	24,071.9	1,538.1	22,533.8	690.4	40.8	649.5	332.4	21.8	310.7	292.8	18.4	274.4
Louisiana	2010	23,441.9	11,280.4	12,161.5	1,186.3	906.4	279.9	824.2	622.1	202.1	635.3	502.7	132.6
Mississippi	2010	30,247.0	13,706.4	16,540.6	1,819.4	1,421.8	397.6	991.7	719.6	272.1	704.7	512.9	191.8
North Carolina	2010	36,633.6	12,595.0	24,038.6	1,561.8	732.1	829.7	1,092.4	616.9	475.5	832.5	502.3	330.2
Oklahoma (east)	2010	7,682.4	1,759.2	5,923.2	197.5	131.0	66.5	138.0	72.6	65.5	86.9	54.1	32.8
South Carolina	2010	23,488.3	11,837.5	11,650.8	1,294.3	886.0	408.3	830.3	607.7	222.6	540.3	398.2	142.2
Tennessee	2010	28,145.0	3,416.9	24,728.1	850.5	146.2	704.3	420.6	87.8	332.8	328.9	60.3	268.6
Texas (east)	2010	17,334.1	9,657.2	7,676.9	779.3	603.9	175.4	717.0	544.0	173.1	537.6	432.2	105.4
Virginia	2010	33,623.9	7,783.7	25,840.2	1,045.5	367.6	677.9	575.0	275.1	300.0	405.3	186.0	219.3
Total		348,053.6	131,475.5	216,578.2	15,105.5	9,045.8	6,059.7	9,735.5	6,371.9	3,363.7	6,862.3	4,525.3	2,337.0

www.ingramcontent.com/pod-product-compliance
Lightning Source LLC
Chambersburg PA
CBHW081234280526
45787CB00006B/2661